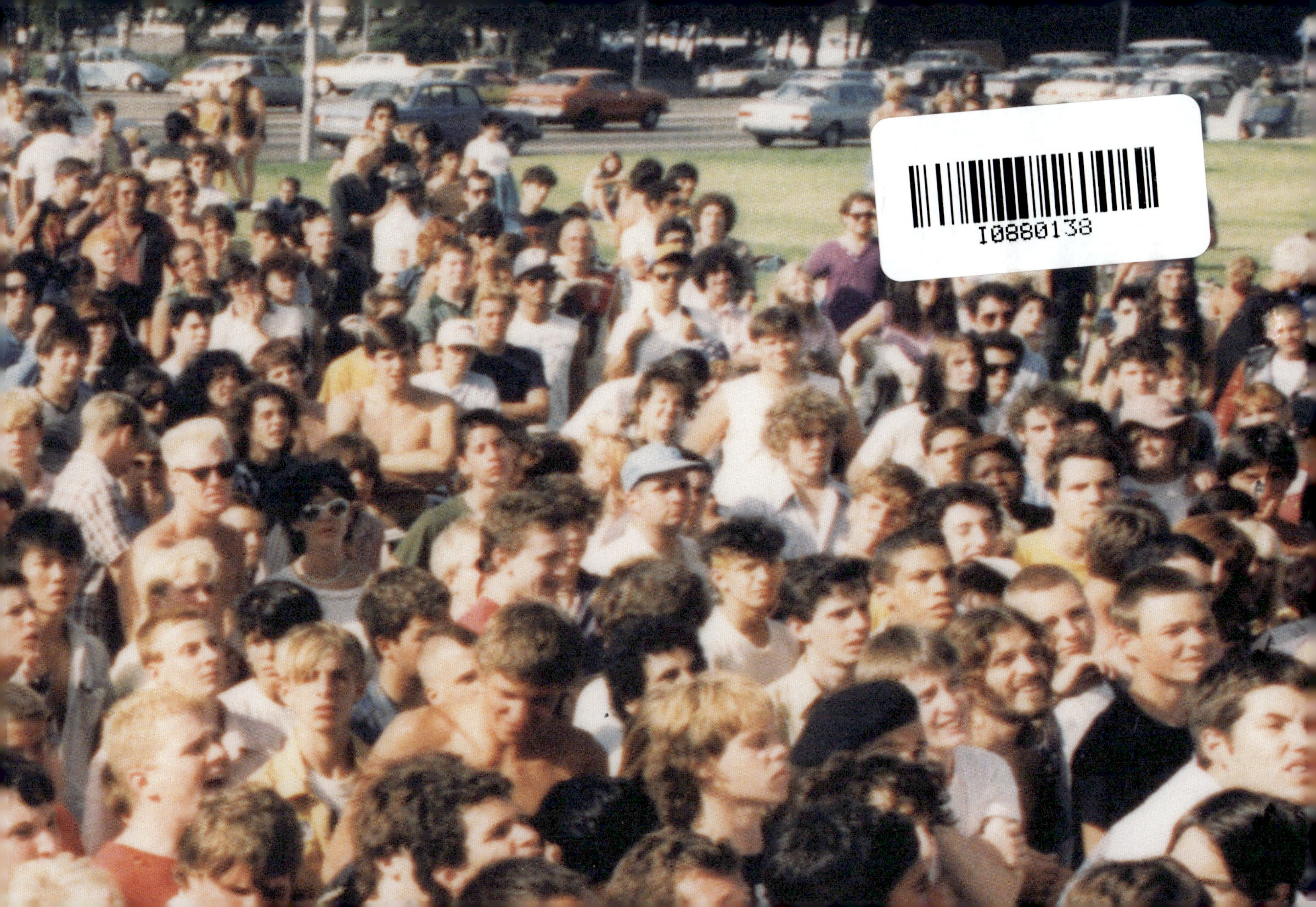

UNITED STATES DEPARTMENT OF JUSTICE

FEDERAL BUREAU OF INVESTIGATION

11000 Wilshire Boulevard
Los Angeles, California, 90024
August 31, 1981

In Reply, Please Refer to
File No. 9A-7053

Honorable Andrea Sheridan Ordin
United States Attorney
U. S. Department of Justice
U. S. Courthouse, Room 1269
Los Angeles, California 90012

RE: Unknown Subjects, doing business as Black Flag; [redacted] doing business as [redacted] - VICTIM
EXTORTION

Attn: Assistant U. S. Attorney
Daniel G. Clement

Dear Ms. Ordin:

On August 19, 1981, Special Agent [redacted] advised Assistant United States Attorney (AUSA) Daniel G. Clement of the results of investigation in captioned matter as follows:

On July 13, 1981, Special Agent [redacted] secured a copy of a cassette recording from radio station

MY WAR ON WILSHIRE

BLACK FLAG vs. the FEDERAL BUILDING ...and the VEX

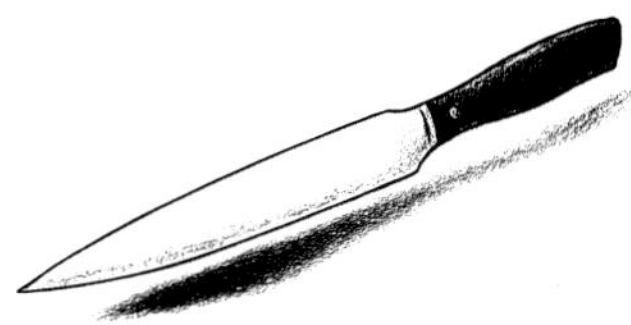

MICHAEL PEARSON

Bazillion Points

MY WAR on WILSHIRE

Black Flag vs. the Federal Building...and the Vex

Bazillion Points

First U.S. printing, 2026

Bazillion Points Books

New York | United States

BAZILLIONPOINTS.com

Bazillion thanks to Michael Pearson, Jordan Schwartz, Steve McDonald, Chris Petersen, Dez Cadena, Kevin Salk, Joe Carducci, Dave Chandler, Henry Rollins, Chuck Dukowski, David O. Jones, Bill Sassenberger, James Lo, and the Freedom of Information Act

Library of Congress Control Number: 2025939131

Library of Congress Cataloging-in-Publication Data is available upon request.

ISBN 978-1-935950-78-3

Printed in China

The authorized representative in the EU for product safety and compliance is:

EAS Europe OÜ, Mustamäe tee 50, 10621 Tallinn, Estonia | easproject.com *for Ben and Jean*

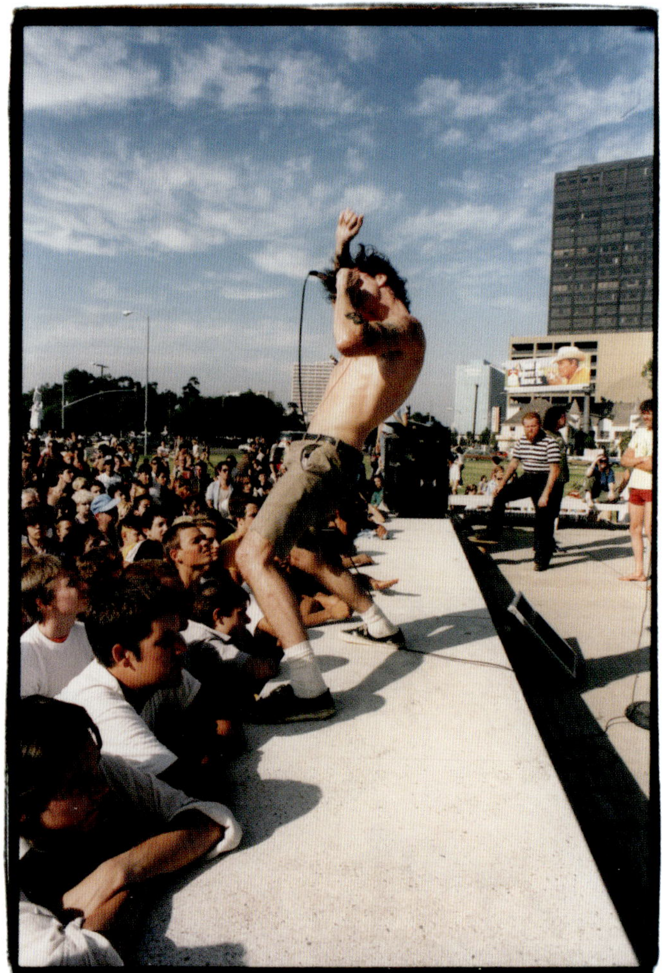

TABLE of CONTENTS

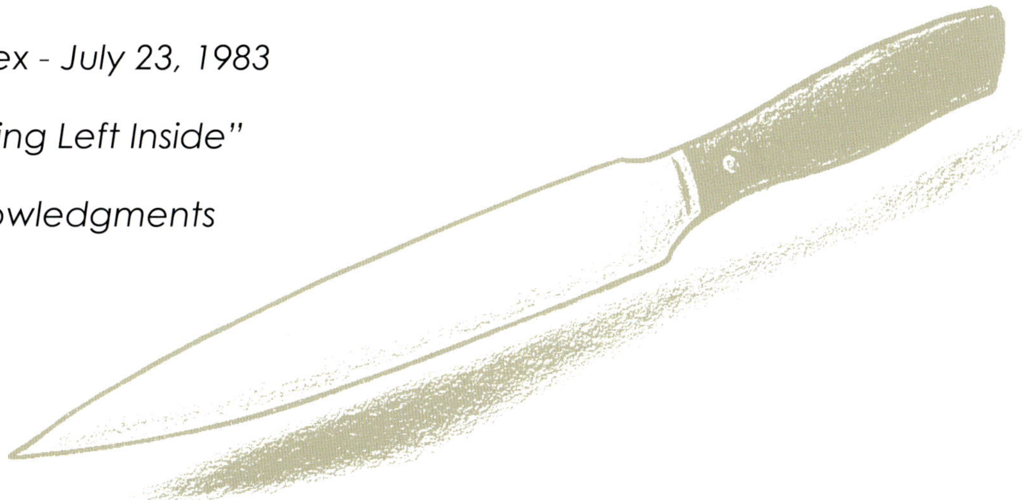

CLOCKED IN

I grew up on the Los Angeles Westside in Pacific Palisades, between Santa Monica and Malibu. My dad was a talent agent who kept old movie stars working in dinner theater as their careers waned. As a kid, I was always into skateboarding and surfing. I skated at times with the Dogtown guys—including Tony Alva, Jay Adams, Stacy Peralta, and Arthur Lake. They'd come skate at the houses of a couple of my friends who had really good backyard half pipes, and at my local skatepark, Marina Del Rey. I started shooting a lot of photos of skateboarding, and making three-minute movies on my Super 8 camera.

I was raised on classic rock such as Led Zep, Hendrix, Alice Cooper, AC/DC, and Rush. Then in 1979, I found out about punk rock from the *L.A. Weekly*, and I started seeing strange-looking new records in local shops. I was blown away. My friend Mark Munsky and I started going to lots of great shows: Devo, Adolescents, Weirdos, Germs, Circle Jerks, X, Ramones, the DKs, and, of course, the mighty Black Flag.

For a while during 1982 and 1983, I played bass in a hardcore band called Armed Response. They recorded a track for the *We Got Power (Party or Go Home)* compilation before I joined. Two punk rock twin brothers, Ken and Rich Waco, started the band, then they had a falling out. I became the bass player for Ken's Armed Response, and Rich had his own Armed

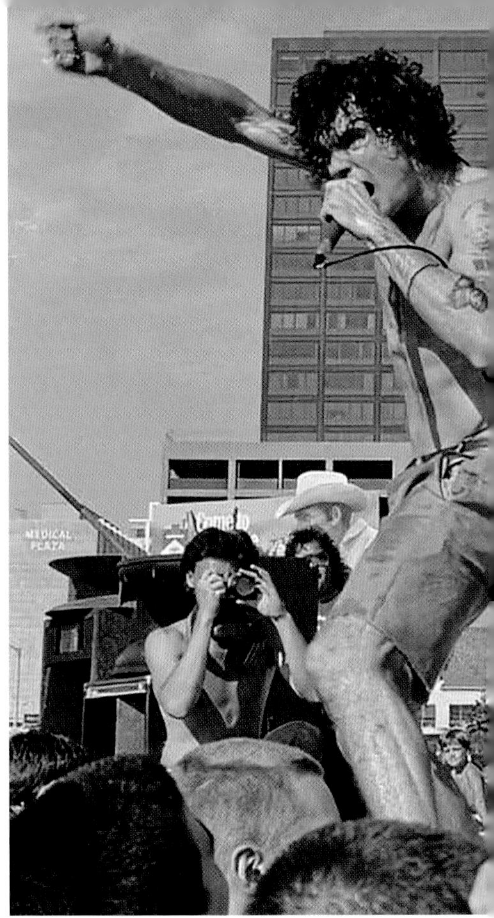

Me on stage, shirtless and 17, shooting photos.

PHOTO BY KEVIN SALK

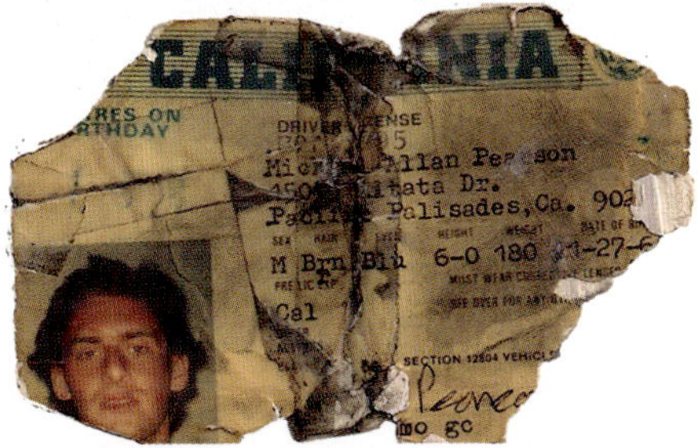

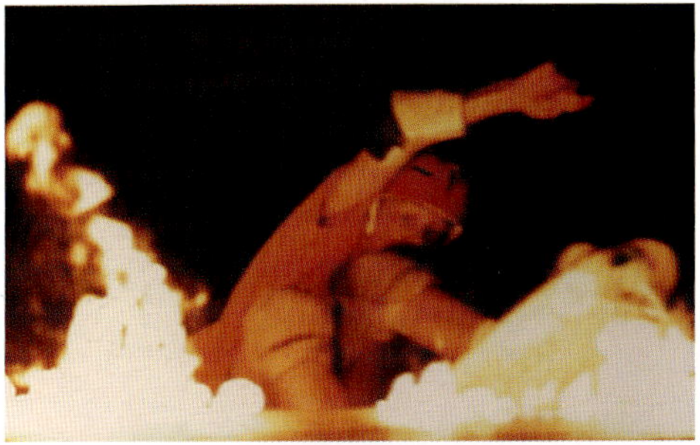

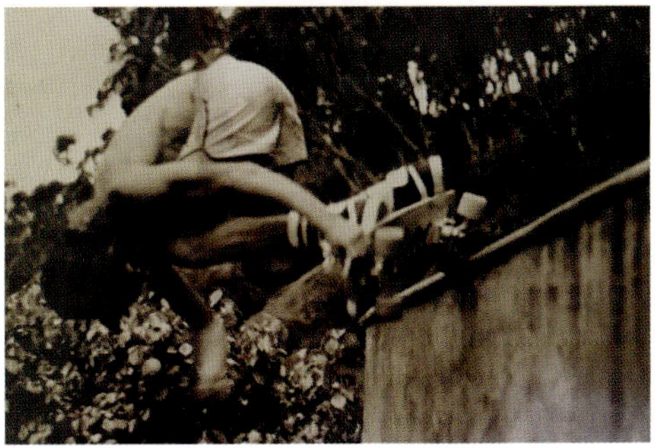

Response. It was pretty ridiculous having two Armed Responses for a while.

I didn't take my Olympus OM-1 camera to many shows. I didn't want to get it smashed in my face—or just plain smashed. I only took it to Black Flag at the Federal Building, and again at the Vex. They were top-echelon hardcore punk, and they were my favorite band. I couldn't resist getting some shots. I wanted to hold onto those moments that were so alive and fun and intense.

I'm sixty now, and I live in Redondo Beach, Black Flag's former home base. A lot has changed. I became a psychotherapist at thirty-five. I enjoy helping people with emotional issues, many of which stem from neglect, loss, and trauma. Our generation experienced a lot of that. I believe that's why kids were drawn to the wild abandon of punk rock. We really got to let loose as hardcore kids back then. It was a great catharsis.

Over the decades, my great interest in skating and punk rock hasn't faded. I've been writing about the hardcore days, I have a few skate videos and such on my YouTube channel: @mikeapearson

I hope you enjoy these pics.

FROM TOP: My driver's license—messed up to hide the birth date. I said it burned in a fire so I could try to buy beers; Steve Olpin on his cement half-pipe in Santa Monica Canyon. We lit it on fire with gasoline. This spot was briefly in Lords of Dogtown; my photo of Tony Alva at Steve Olpin's ramp.

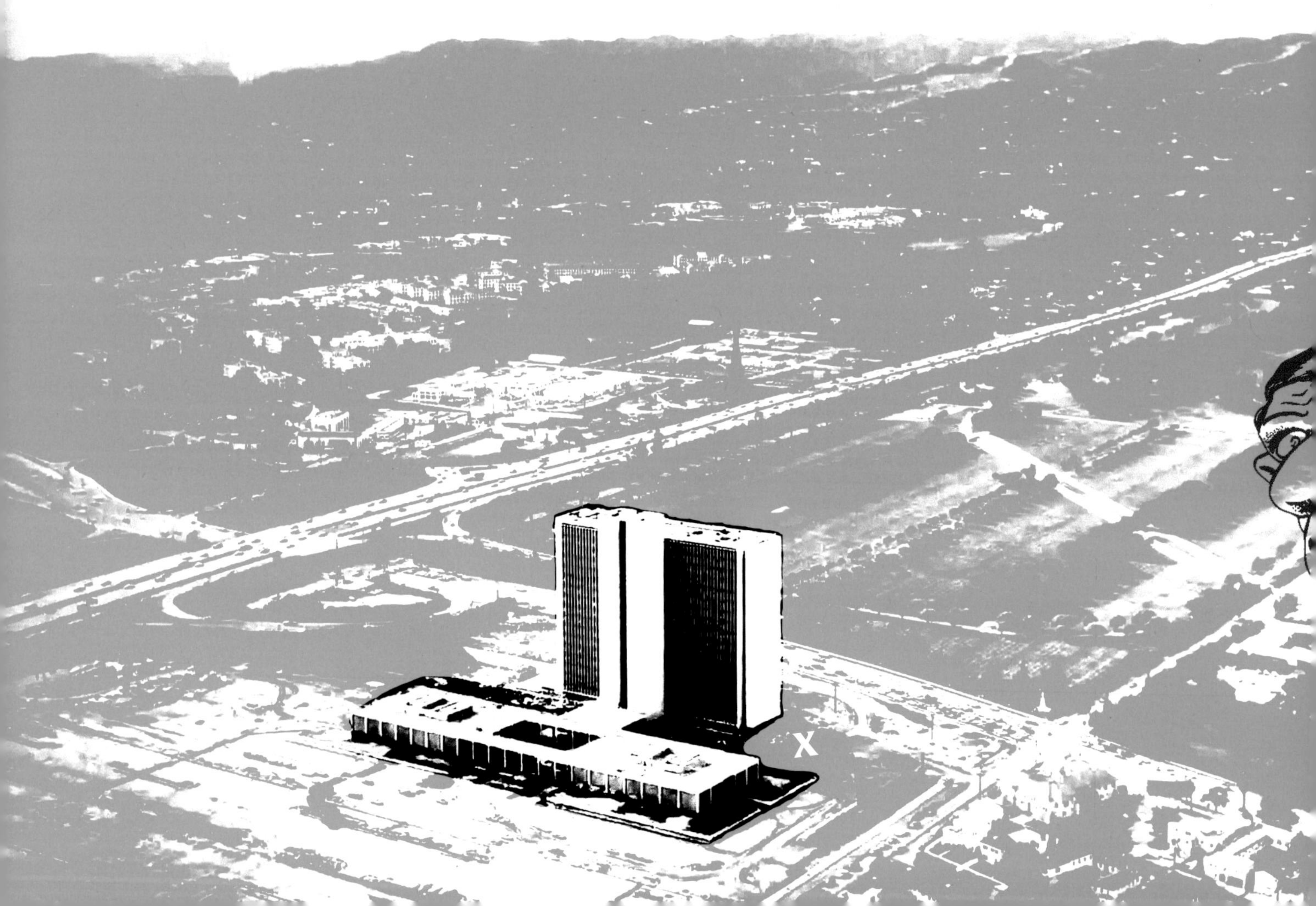
X

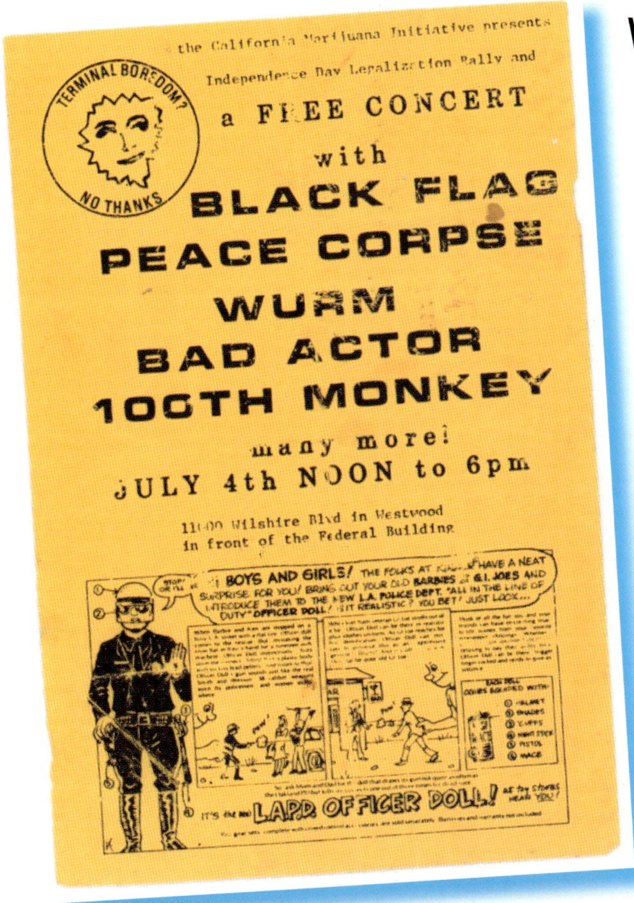

Wilshire Federal Building
11000 Wilshire Blvd.
July 4, 1983

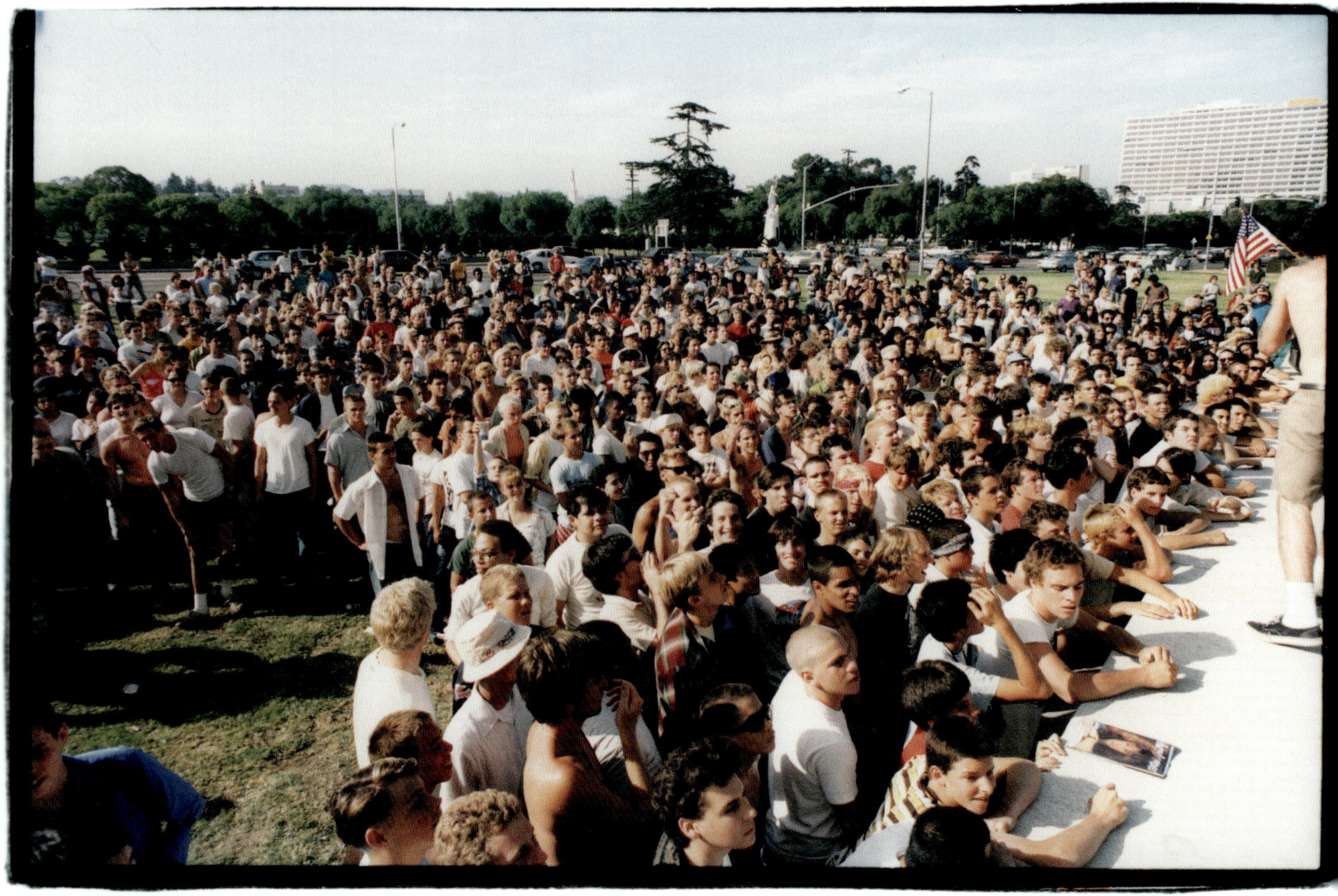

FOREVER TIME

Black Flag's show on July 4, 1983, at the Federal Building in Westwood was a free "legalize weed" benefit, of all things. The band was in a desperate era during its involuntary recording hiatus following the release of *Damaged* in 1981. This period was probably the peak of Black Flag, full of dividing lines.

For one, since the debut Black Flag had slowed down their sound, making it kind of Black Sabbath-like—very heavy, but with more weird strange dissonant sounds. They played memorable new songs including "My War," "Black Coffee," "Slip It In," and "Can't Decide." None of them were released on records until the following year.

Greg Ginn was reportedly smoking a lot of weed at the time. He was definitely noodling some abstract, atonal, and weird leads at this show. He was also wearing a Grateful Dead shirt, which was confusing to a lot of punks. They wondered if it was ironic—it wasn't. Ginn actually loved the Grateful Dead as much as he seemed to love weed.

The two bands had a lot in common. Both began as cutting-edge, countercultural California bands, both cultivated devoted followings, and both toured relentlessly. Black Flag had an incredible work ethic and—again, like the Dead—were always on the road playing shows. They were also open to breaking apart their songs and stretching them out.

To us, Black Flag embodied the DIY ethos of hardcore punk. The Ramones and the Sex Pistols both had major label distribution. Black Flag started their own label out of necessity. They helped pave the way for Dischord Records, Touch and Go, and countless other hardcore labels. They got down to business and did what they needed to do.

For the time, Black Flag was hardcore and frenzied, more intense and crazy than the Ramones, and more raw and wild than the Sex Pistols. I'm sure both of those bands, along with the Stooges, inspired Black Flag, but Black Flag had surpassed them in power and intensity.

In 1983, kids saw the changes in Black Flag and the influence of bands—the Grateful Dead and many others—that eventually opened their minds to different music. Kids branched out from being just into hardcore punk rock. In just a few years, punk mellowed into a revival of hippie rock mixed with a more "alternative" sensibility. I can't forget or forgive the sad and desperate Guns 'N' Roses-inspired guitar rock that came out of so many once-great punk bands.

This benefit for marijuana legalization seemed a bit absurd at the time. Before the bands, the speakers on stage were telling personal stories about going to prison for dealing with pot. Even kids at my high school had gone to jail for selling weed. We thought it would be decades, or never, before marijuana was legalized in California. On July 4, 1983, that kind of acceptance for everything that happened on this Independence Day was still far, far away.

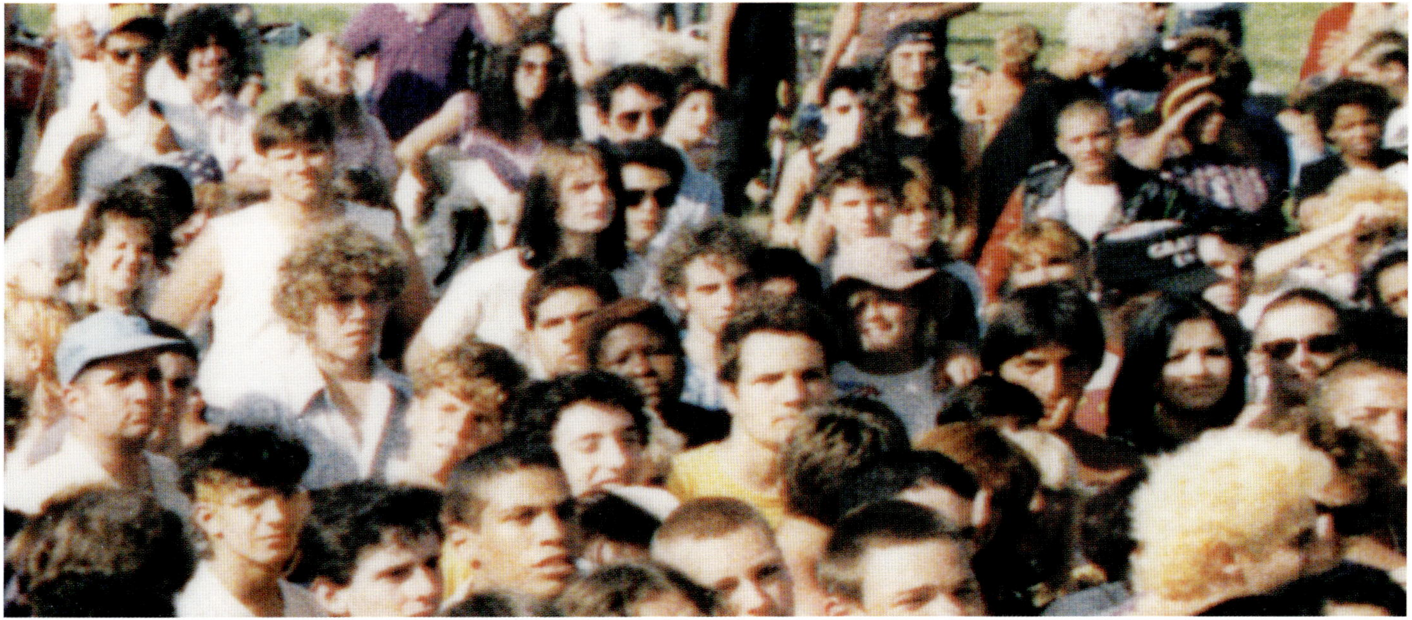

FACES IN THE CROWD

Among the contemporary 1983 details—cars, buildings, Marlboro billboard—the photos offer a rare gathering in broad daylight of the 1983 L.A. hardcore punk scene. In this crowd snippet are: Dez Cadena (top center in backwards cap), who had left Black Flag months earlier. "My recently former band invited me to sing 'Louie Louie' with them at this show"; Steven McDonald of Redd Kross (center left, growing out a black dye job). "I did the math, that's me at sixteen"; prolific photographer Naomi Petersen (center right, jet-black hair); and the *WE GOT POWER!* zine crew (lower center: Jordan Schwartz, David Markey, Jennifer Schwartz, and Kim Pilkington). Also visible elsewhere with cameras are photographers Kevin Salk and Glen E. Friedman.

CMI - THE CALIFORNIA MARIJUANA INITIATIVE

An onstage banner reads "CMI '84," referencing the attempt before the 1984 election to gather signatures, mobilize, and revive California's failed 1970s legalization ballot measure.

"Tomorrow morning, I get the privilege of going to jail for thirty days over at Terminal Island. Most of these fellows here were arrested with me. At one time or another we've been arrested and convicted somewhere else, all for doing demonstrations for CMI over the years." —Stage announcer

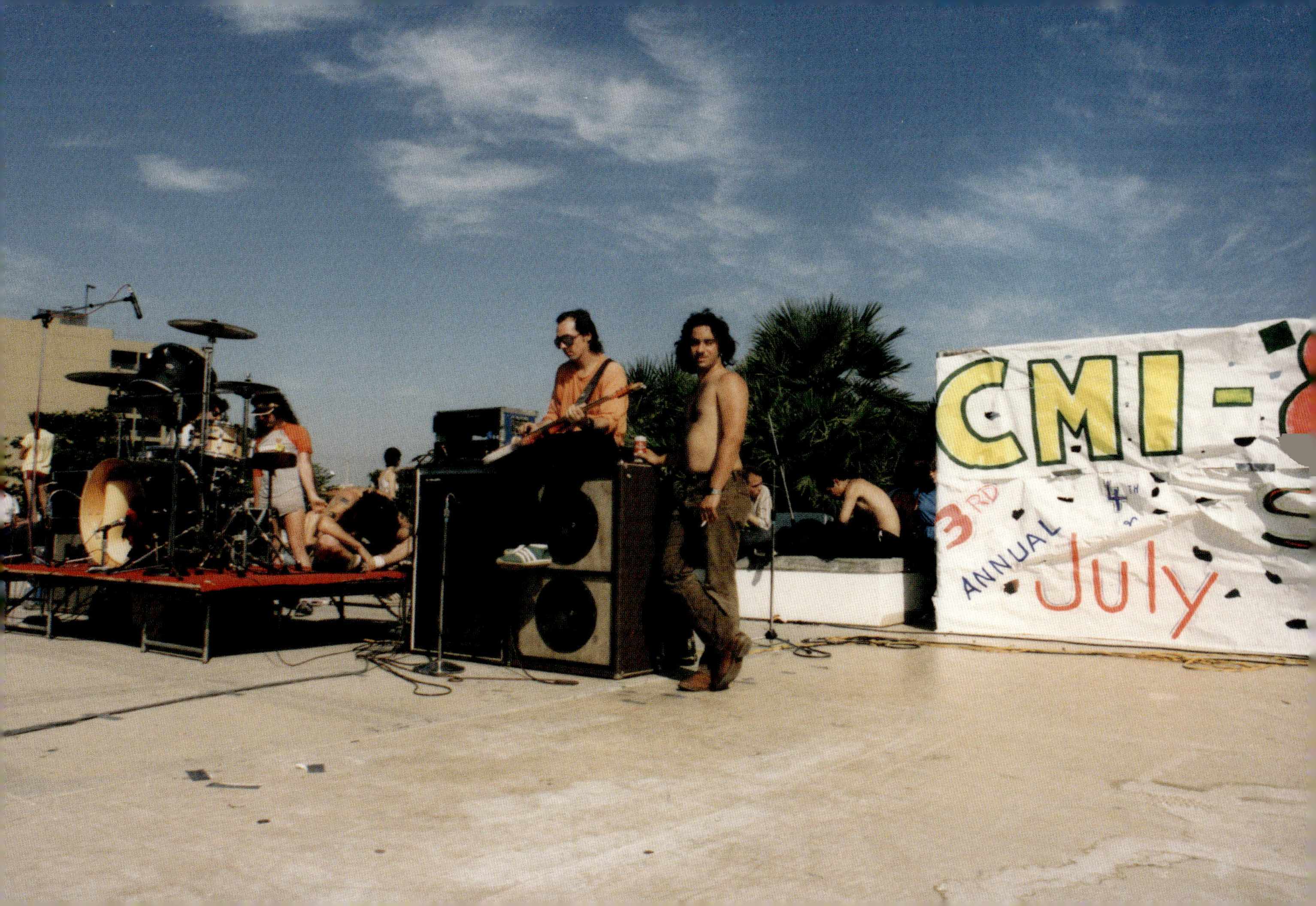
CMI-
3RD ANNUAL
4TH
July

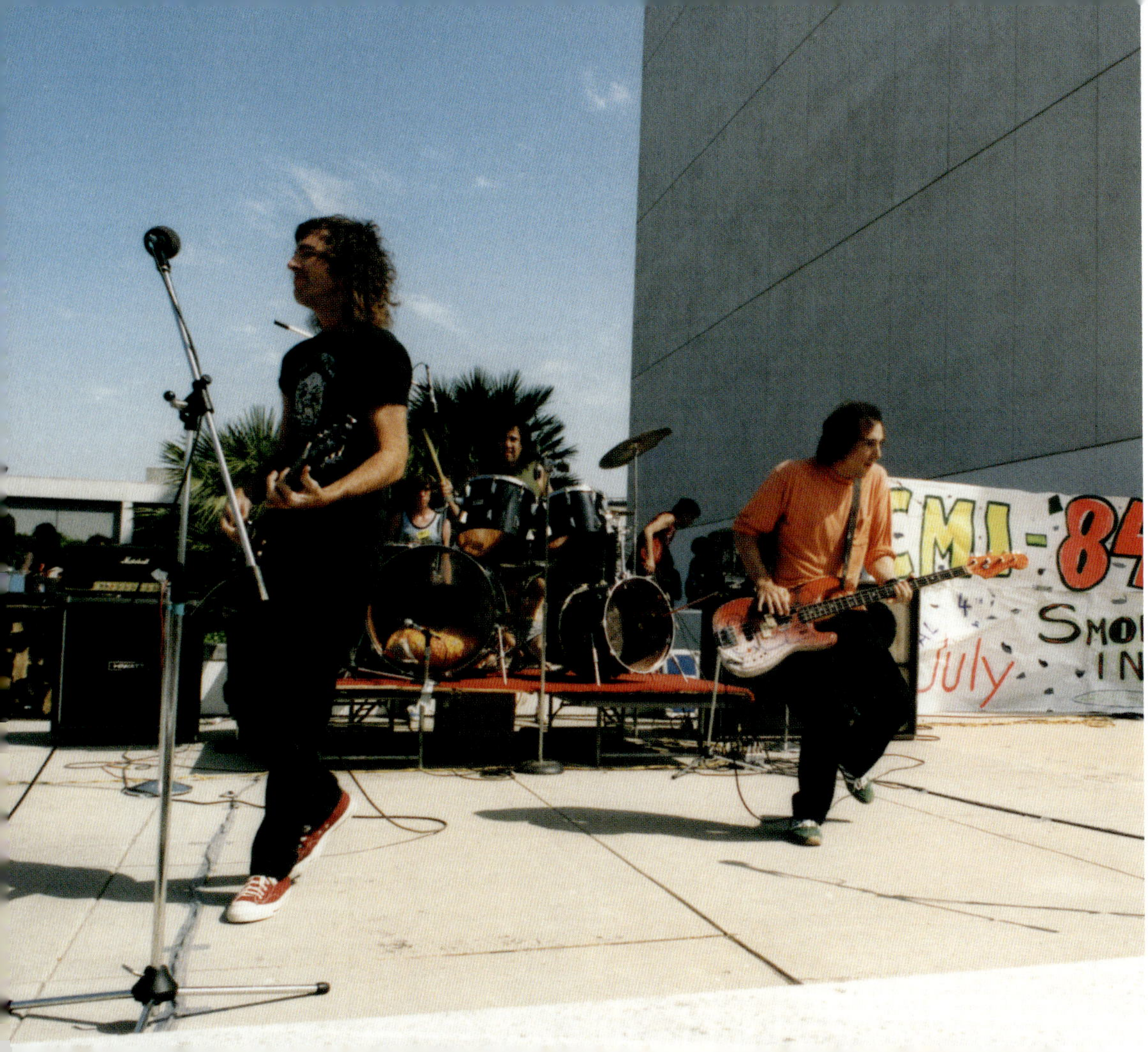

WÜRM

Ed Danky - vocals/guitar

Loud Lou Hinzo - drums

Chuck Dukowski - bass

Formed in Hermosa Beach in 1972, Würm were active until 1977, the year Chuck Dukowski joined Black Flag. During Black Flag's forced hiatus in 1982, Würm reformed and recorded a single as a trio.

The climax of their short set was a feedback-soaked version of the Chambers Brothers' "Time Has Come Today," the '60s rave-up also covered by Angry Samoans and the Ramones.

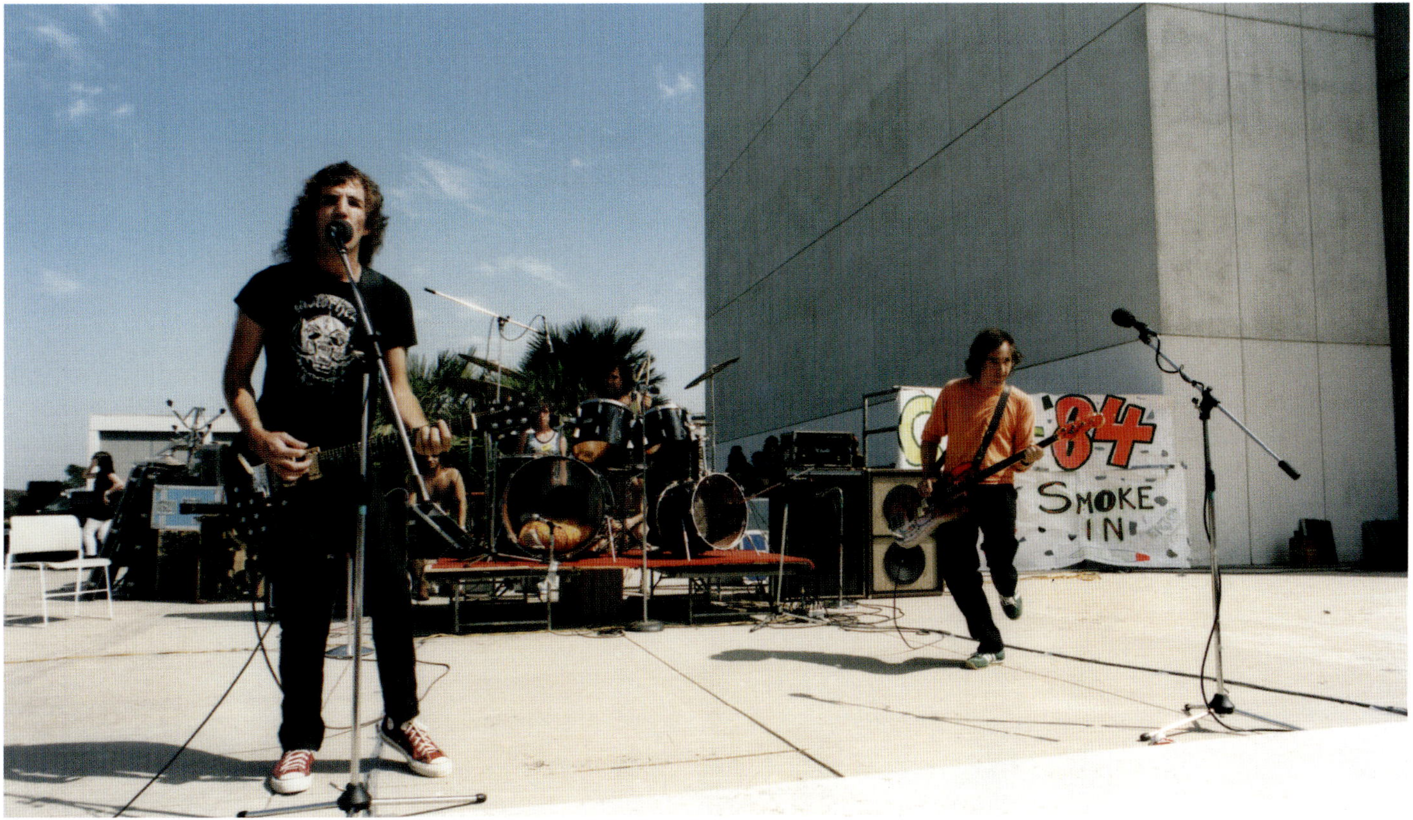
'84
SMOKE
IN

BLACK FLAG

In July 1983, Black Flag was:

Henry Rollins - vocals

Greg Ginn - guitars

Bill Stevenson - drums

Chuck Dukowski - bass

Dave Claassen - backing vocals

Dez Cadena - guest vocals

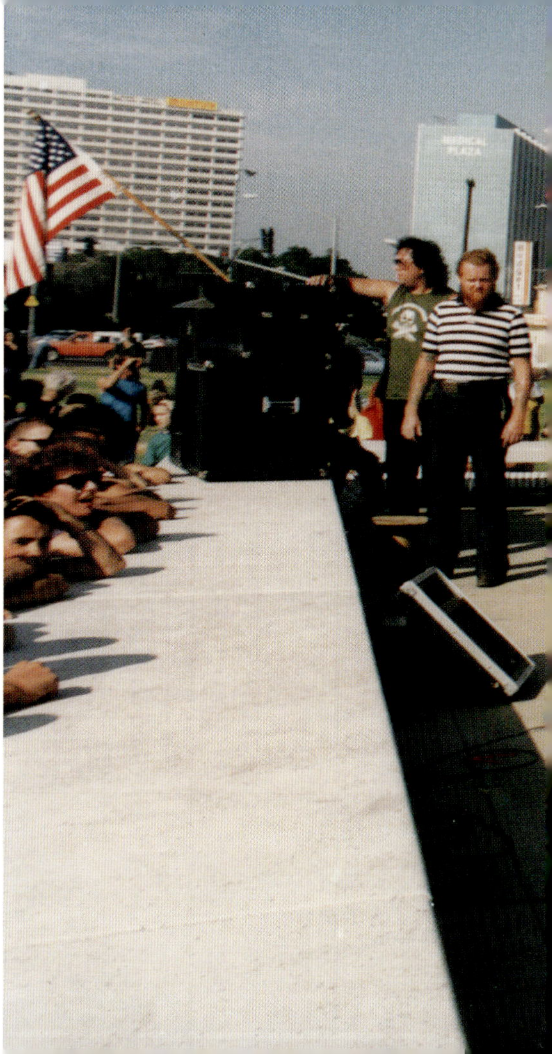

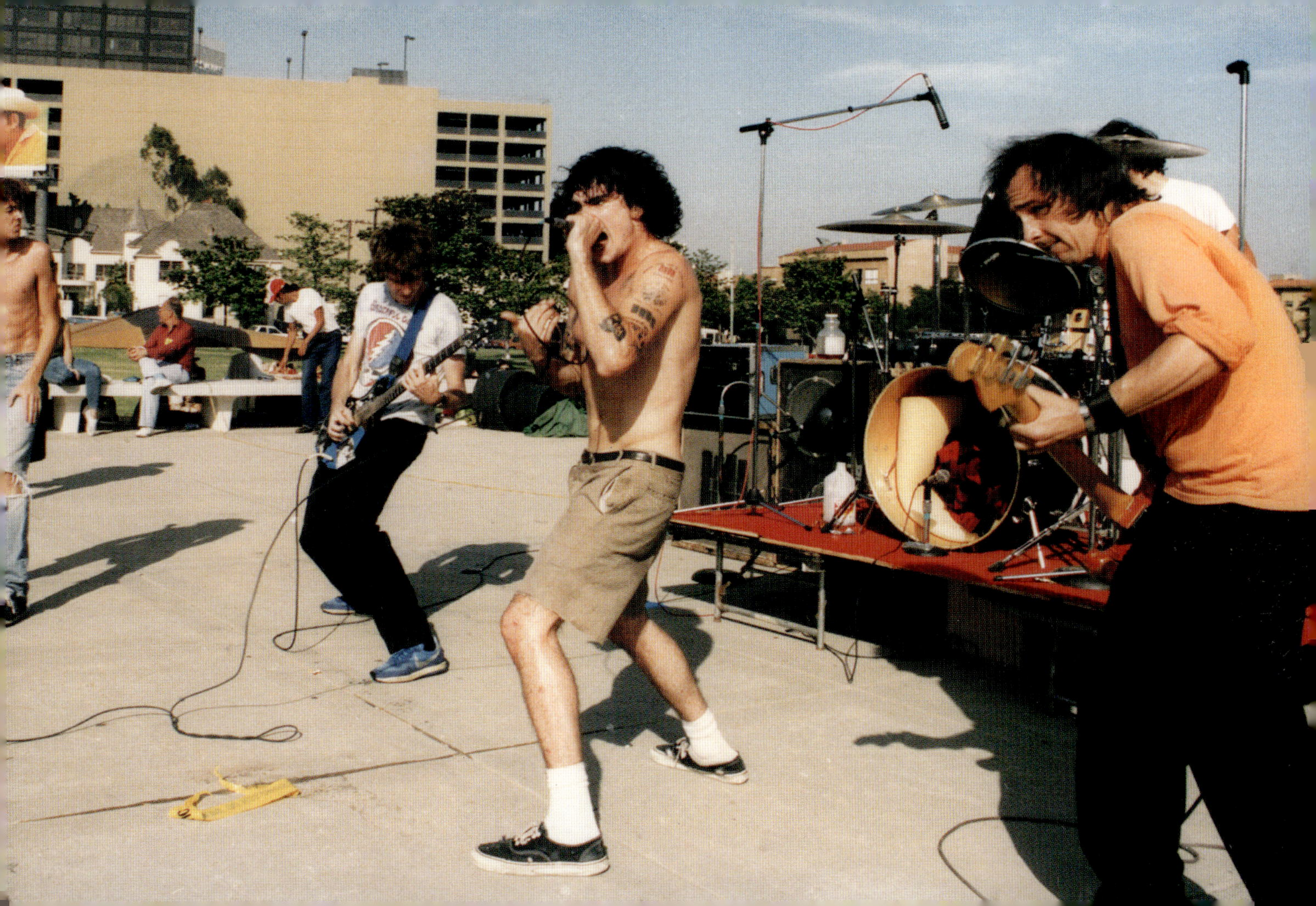

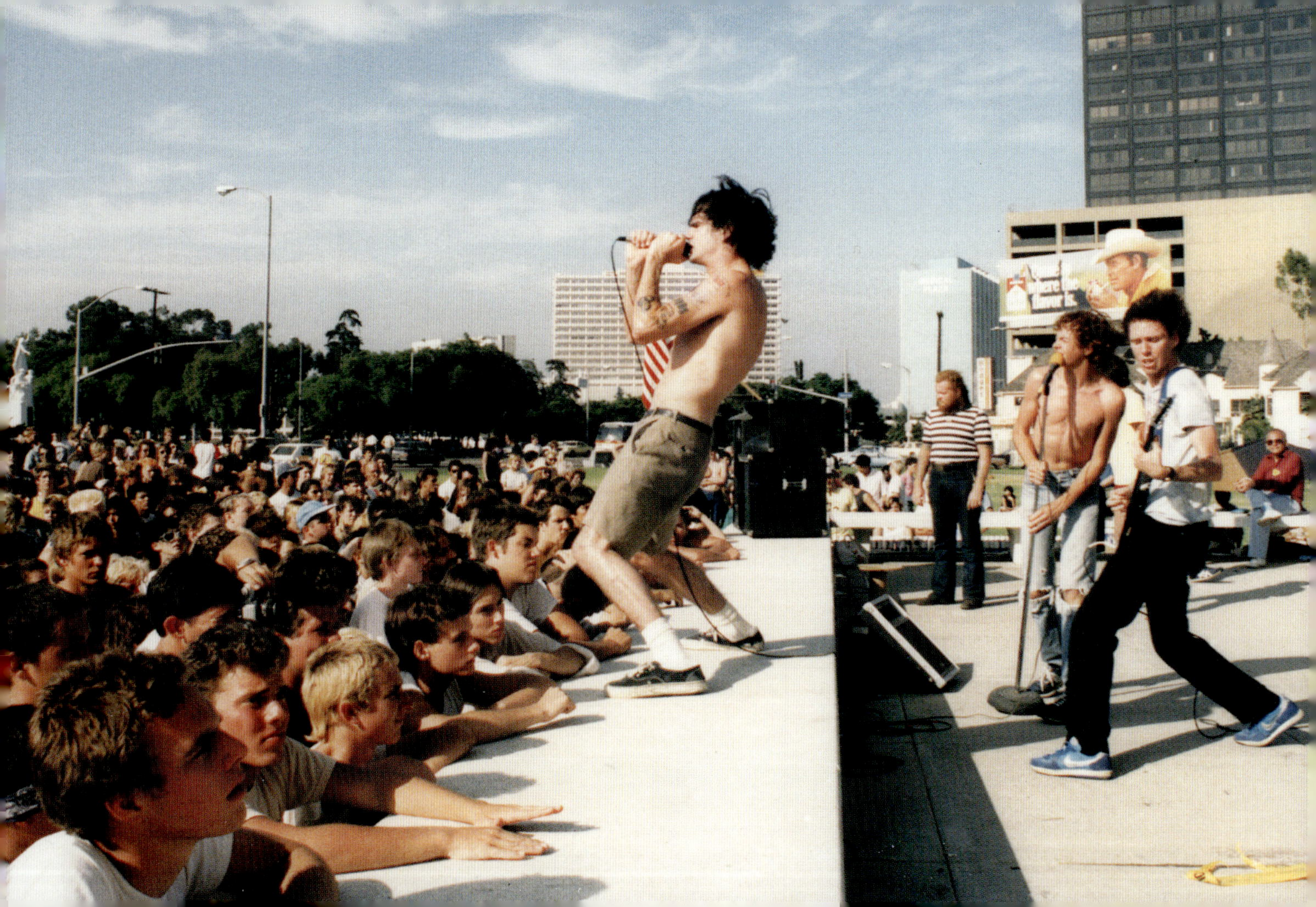

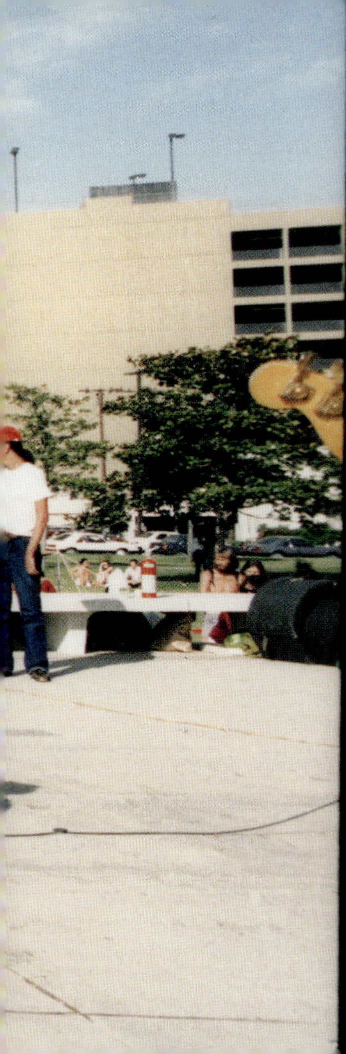

"Okay, now I'm gonna make some long speeches now about how cops are icky and how pot rules, so you guys all like me and shit!"

"Hey, we're talkin' summer '83, this is cool city... This is kind of like the US Festival, it's like the 'Pus Festival'!"

"Any money that gets thrown up here will be donated to a pretty cool cause. We're going to be saving some whales. We're going to be saving D. Boon, he's a pretty cool whale.

"Hey, can you guys throw us some joints up here?"

—Henry Rollins stage taunts

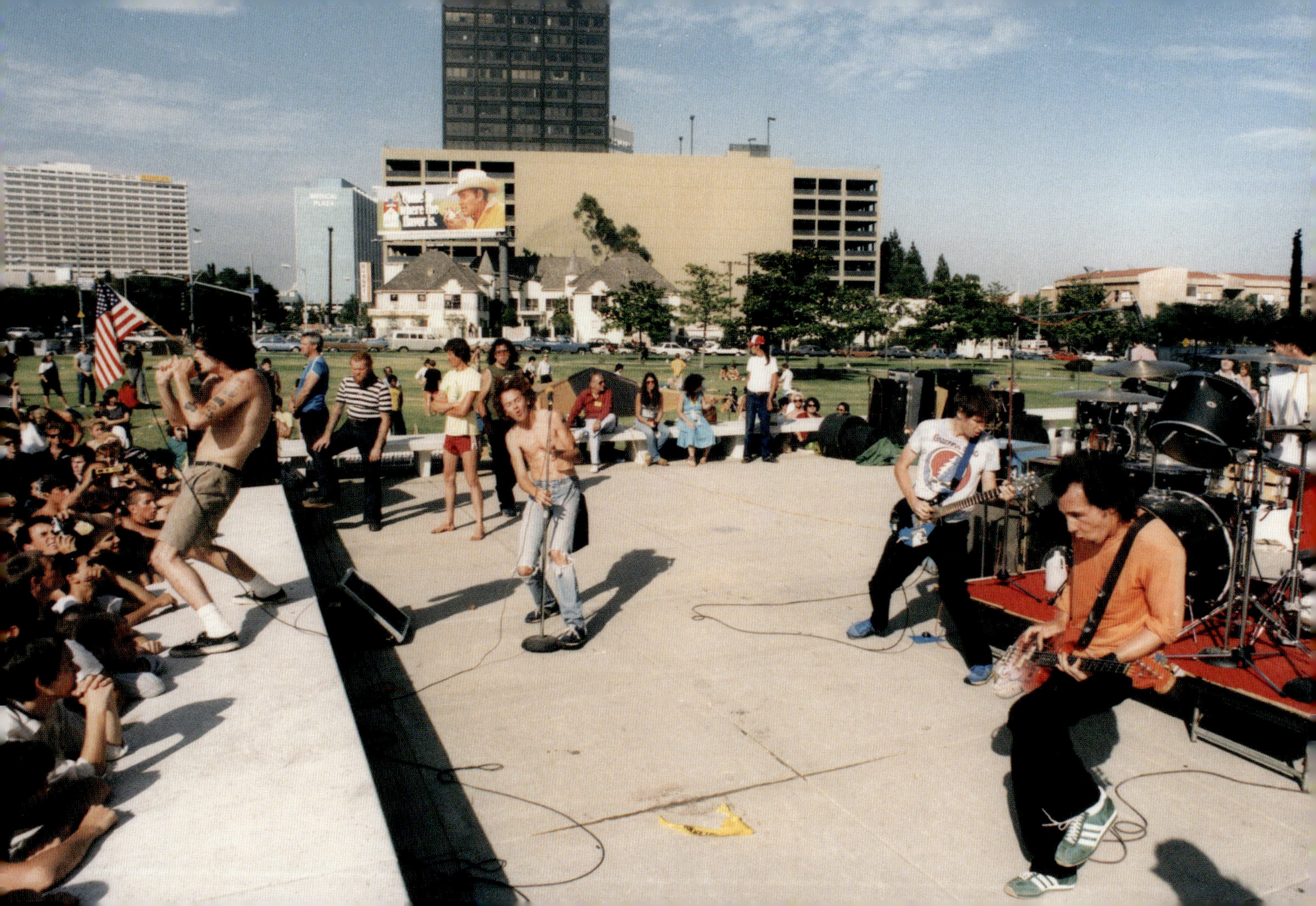

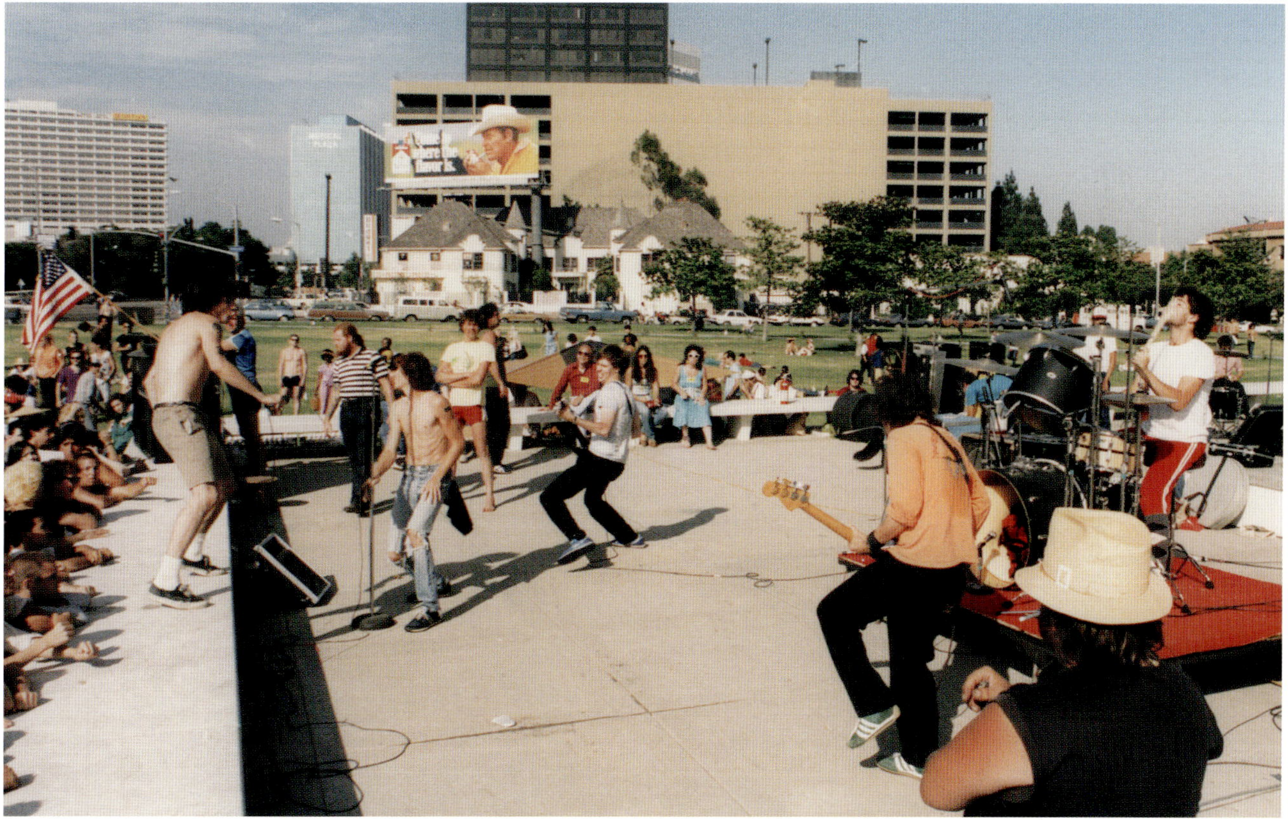

LEGALIZING BLACK FLAG

"My band Peace Corpse was on the bill. I was actually a veteran of pot rallies. I had tried to get arrested in front of the White House in 1978, way before legalization. Most of those things involved live rock bands, but still it was just weird seeing punks involved in a pro-marijuana event.

"My friend Steve Morris had invited Black Flag to play this smoke-in. He called Greg Ginn with the idea, knowing the band was pretty much blacklisted during this time from playing other L.A. clubs."

—Bill Sassenberger, Peace Corpse/Toxic Shock Recs.

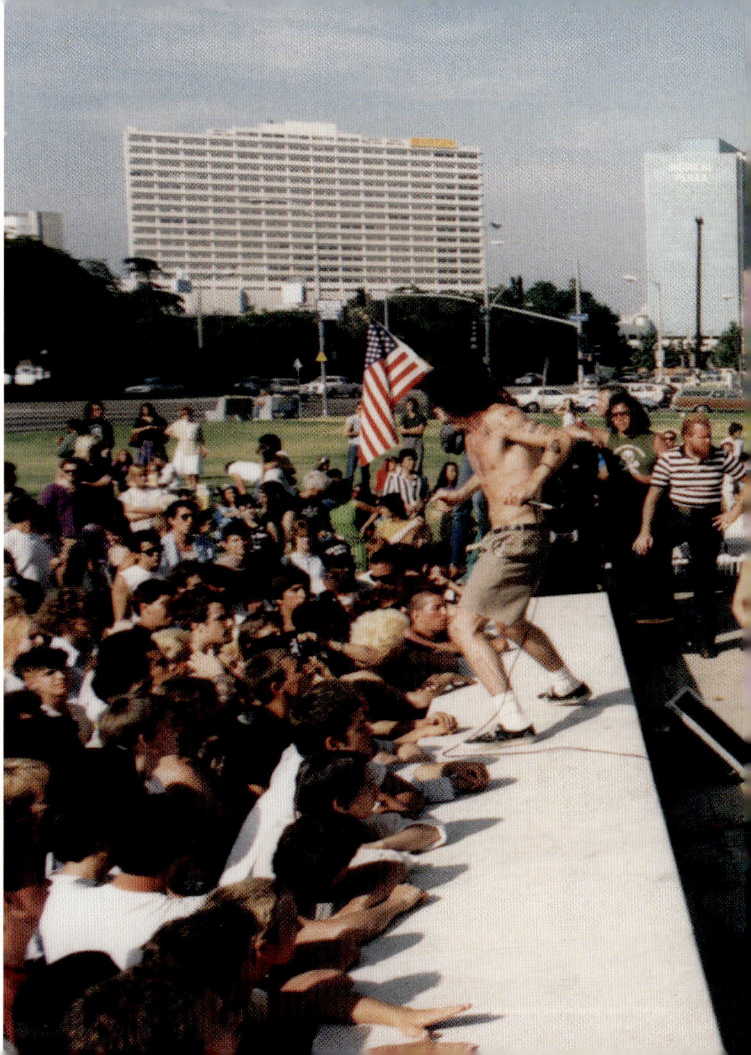

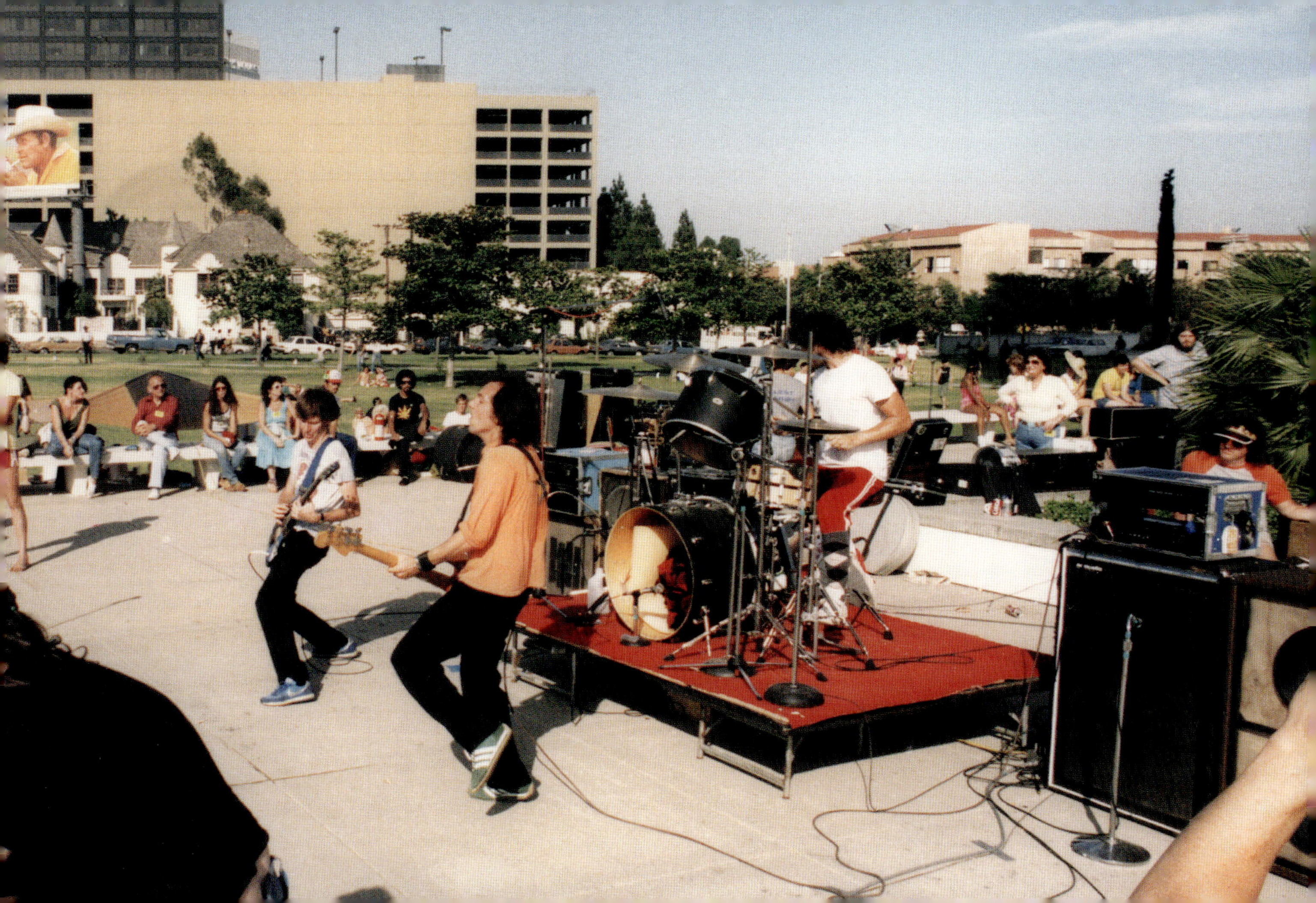

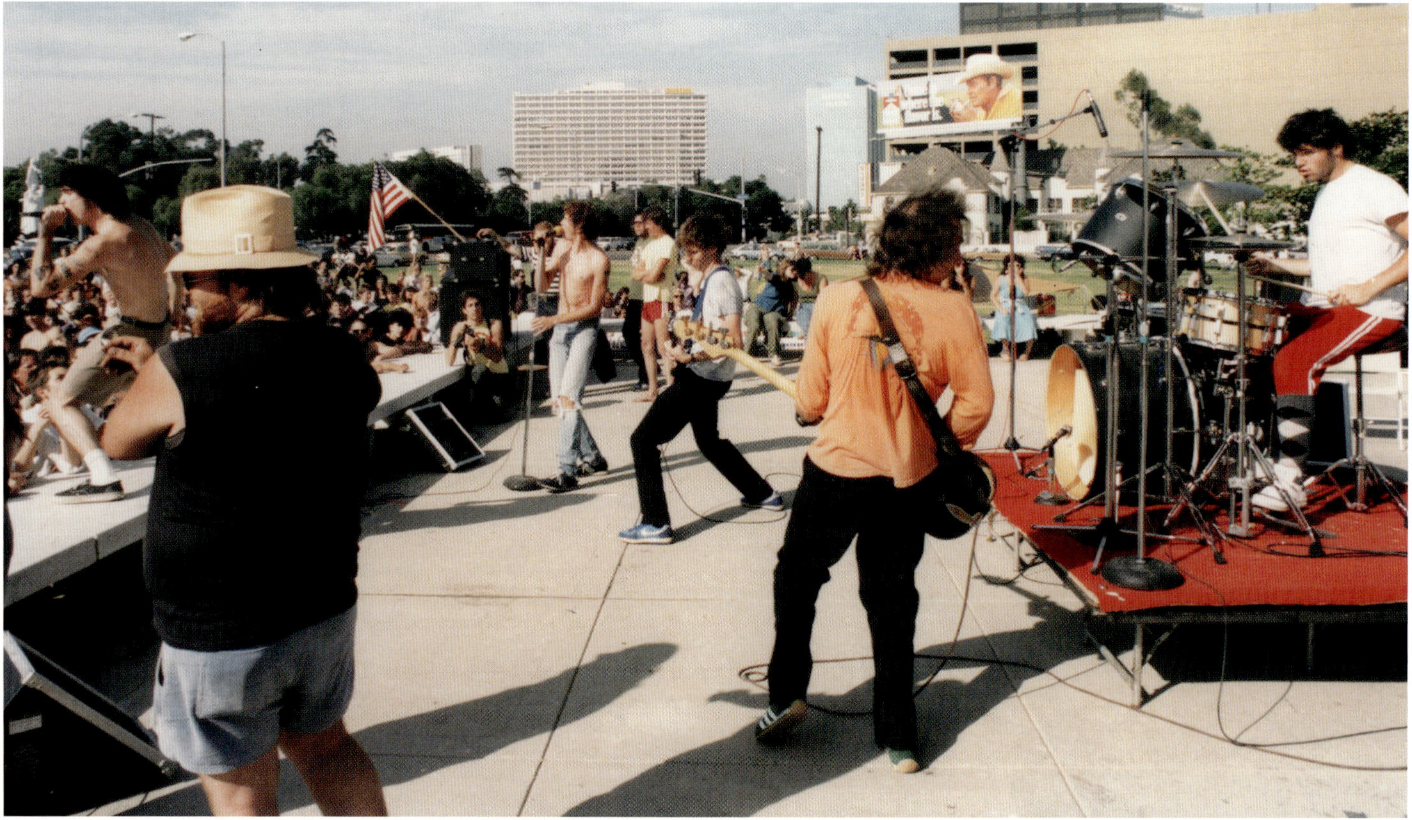

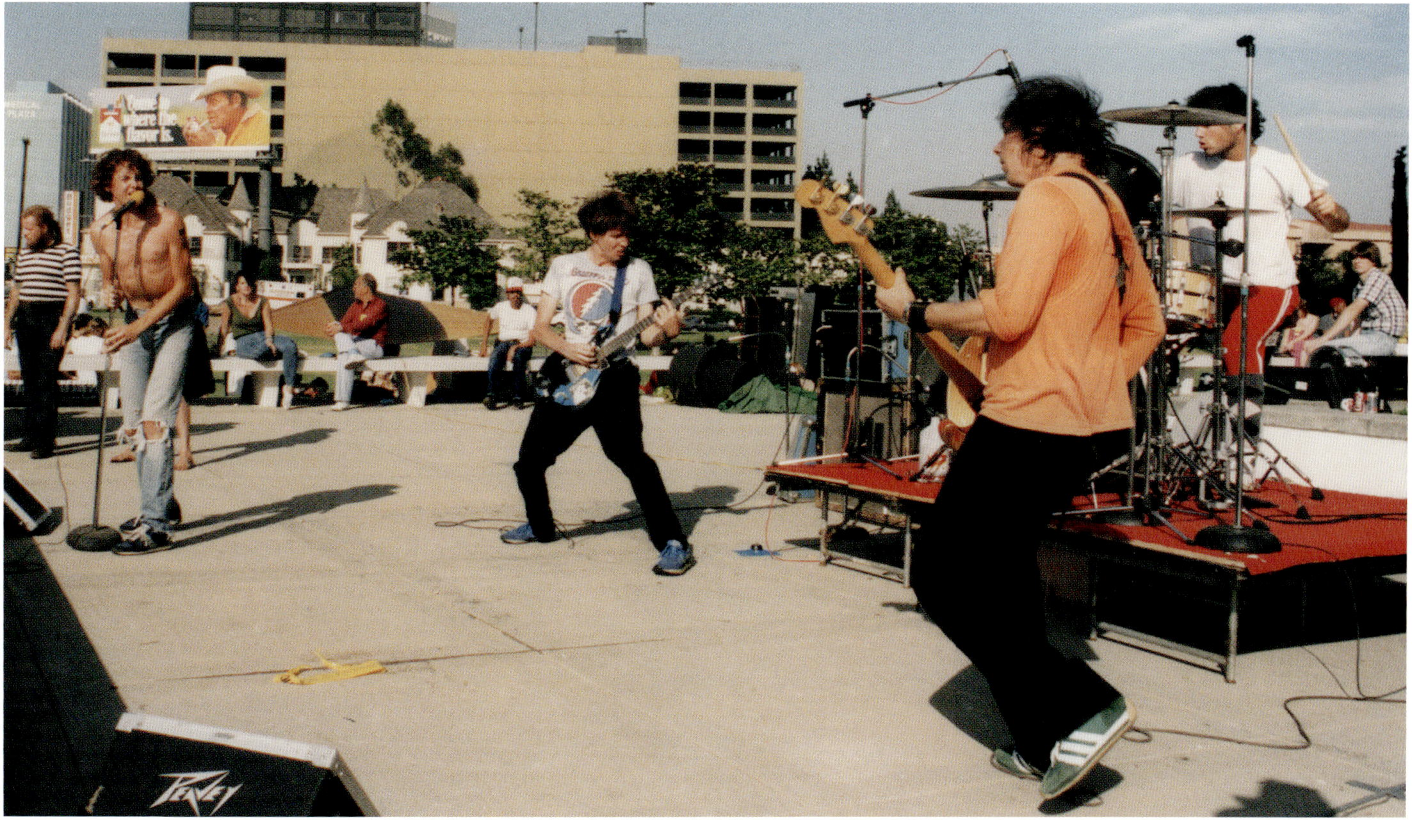

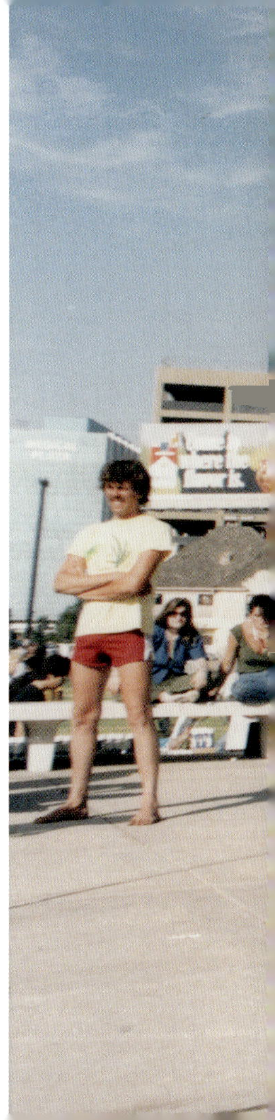

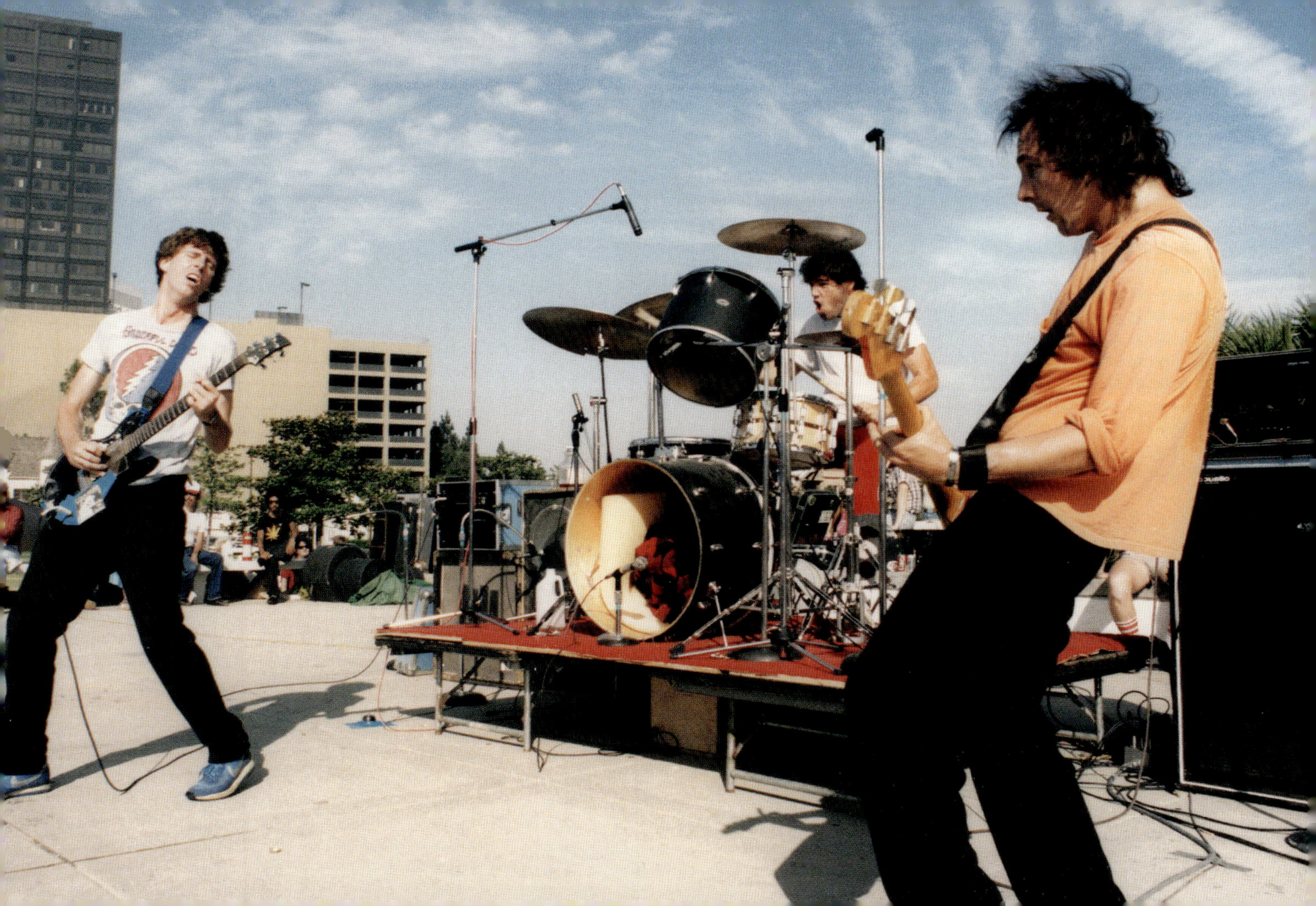

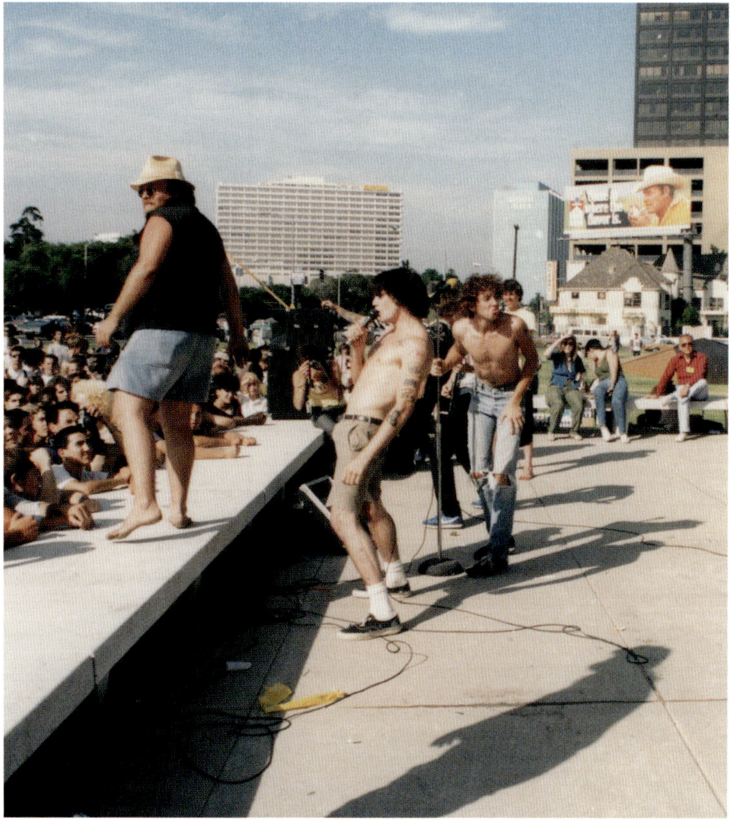

SO-CAL SECURITY

The barefoot and bearded marijuana legalization supporters acting as security were not prepared for the Black Flag crowd. Though the audience was unusually mellow—probably due to lack of beer—they were still hard to handle. The tattered yellow police barricade tape on the stage had initially been stretched across the front of the terrace to prevent stage diving.

"There was a big chasm between the potheads and any cultural activity in those years."—Joe Carducci

"Hang tight, calm down! We've had people been here from the fire department, they said they would shut us down if we set off any more firecrackers or fireworks, so please mellow out on those. And please don't come all the way here on stage. Don't cross this barrier, just come up and dive just back in and we'll be cool."
—Stage announcer

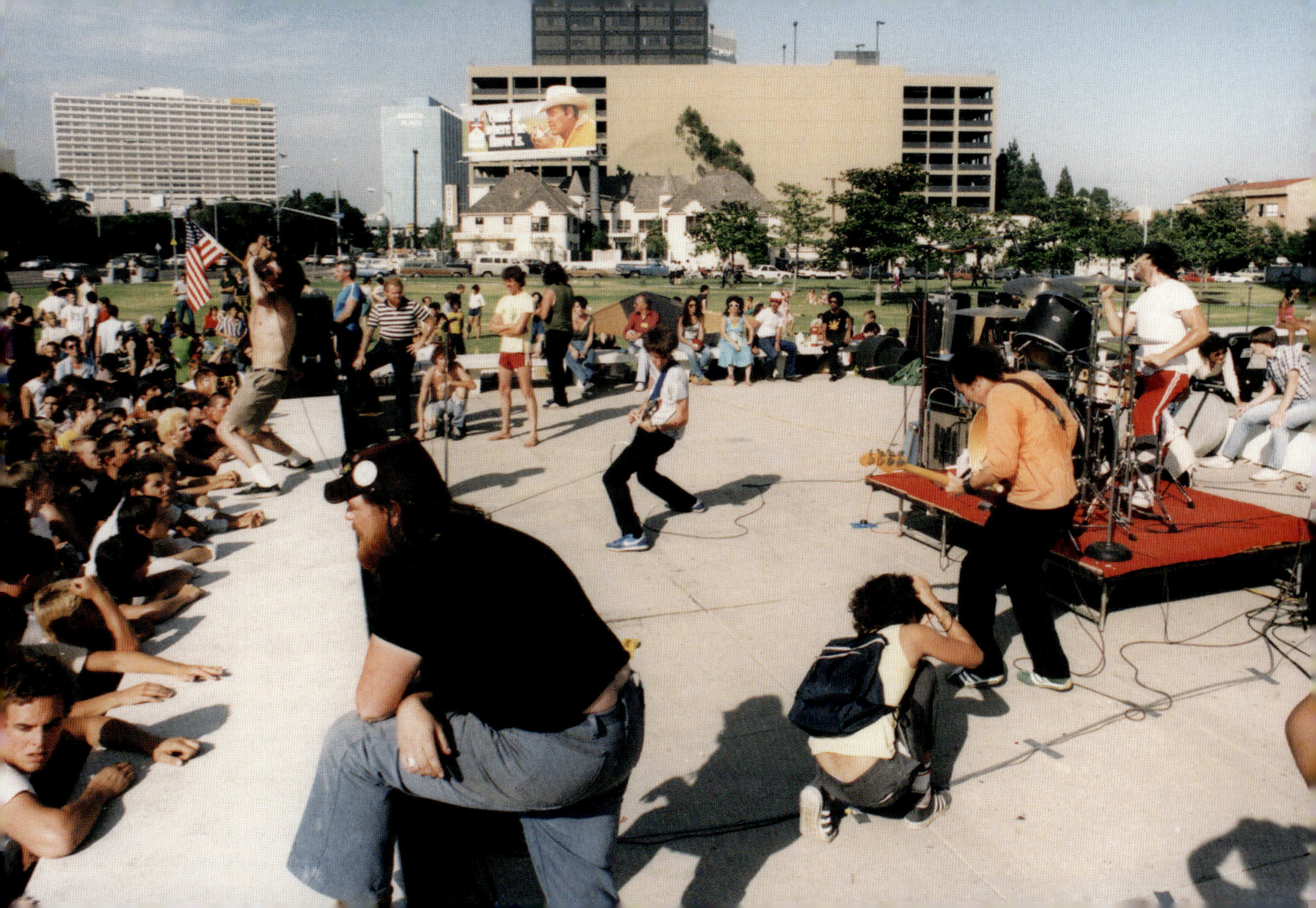

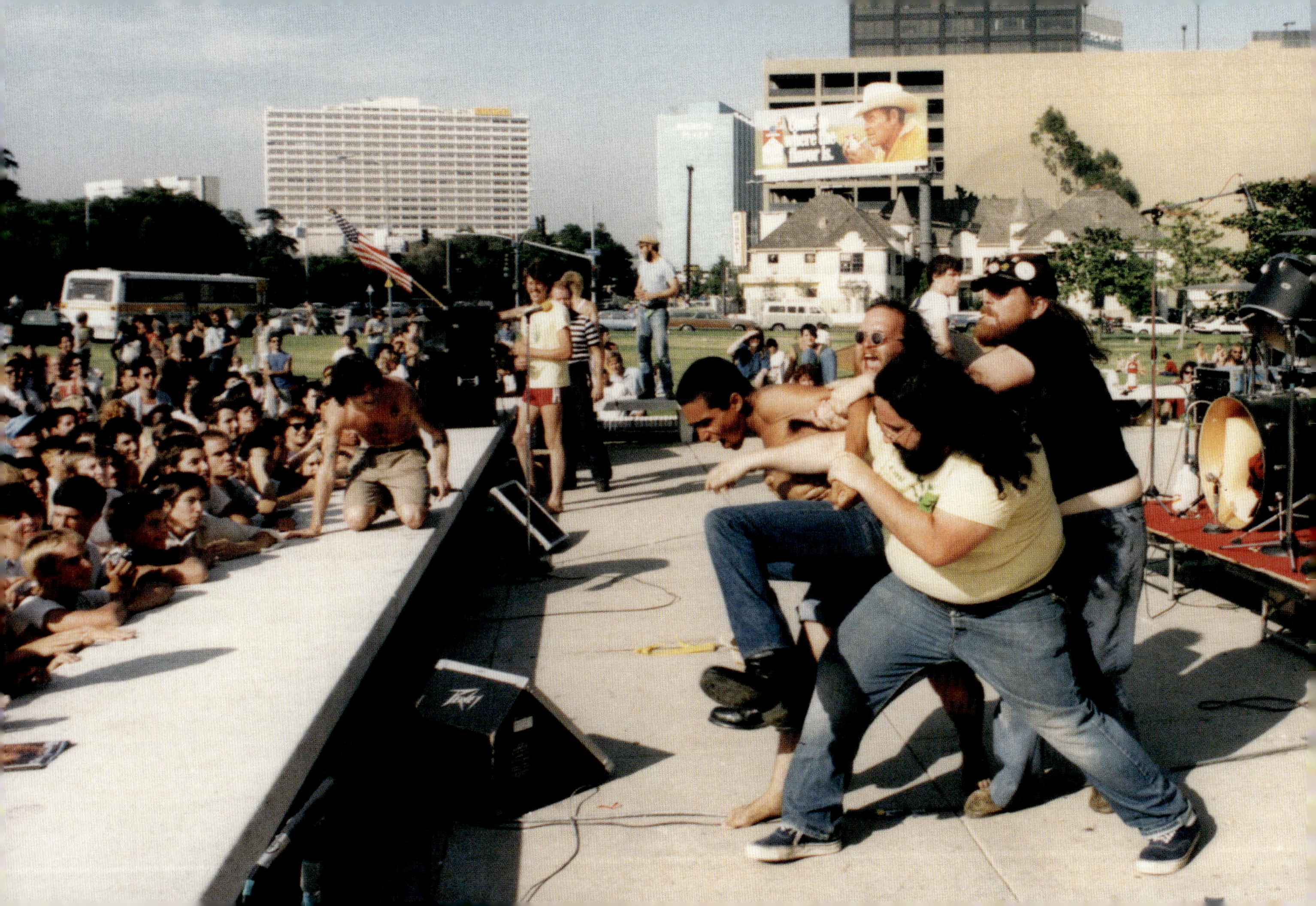

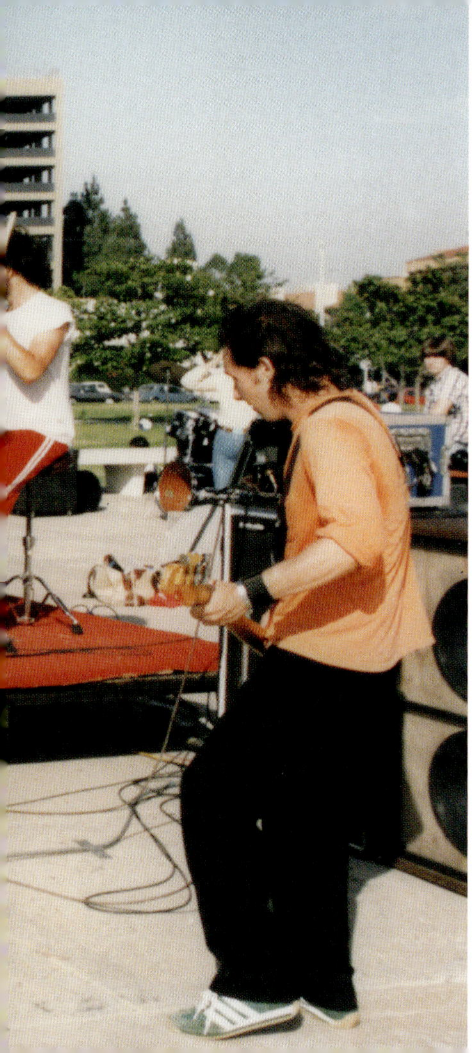

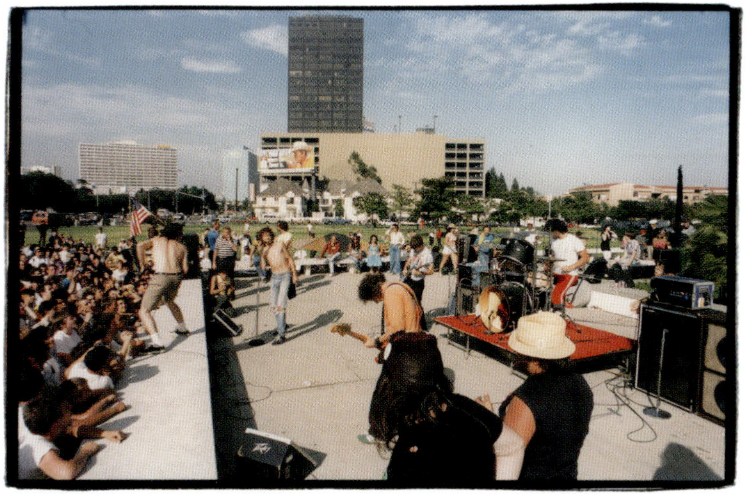

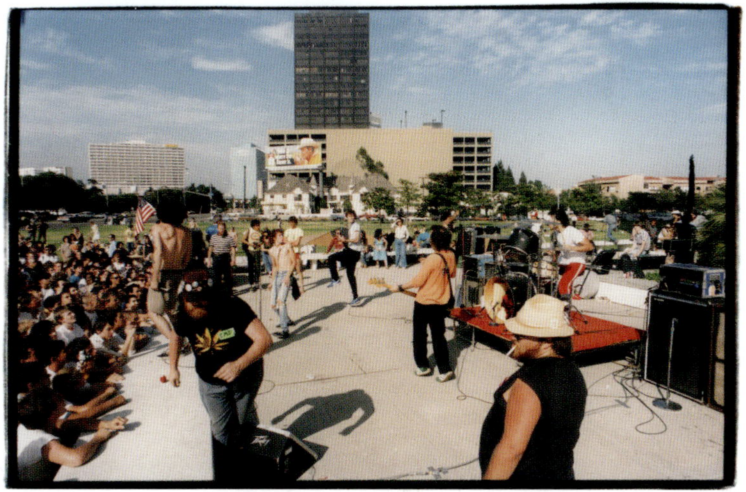

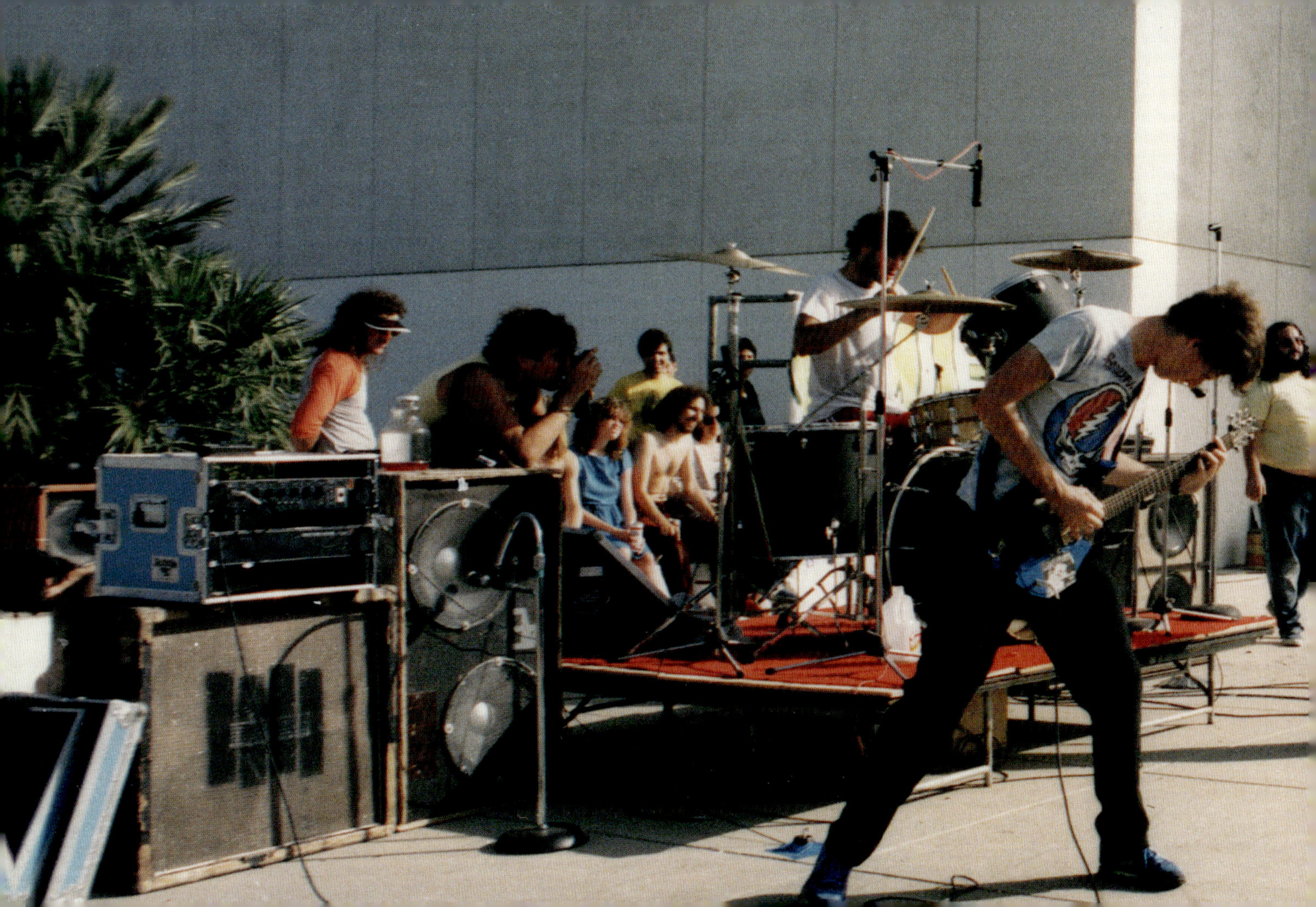

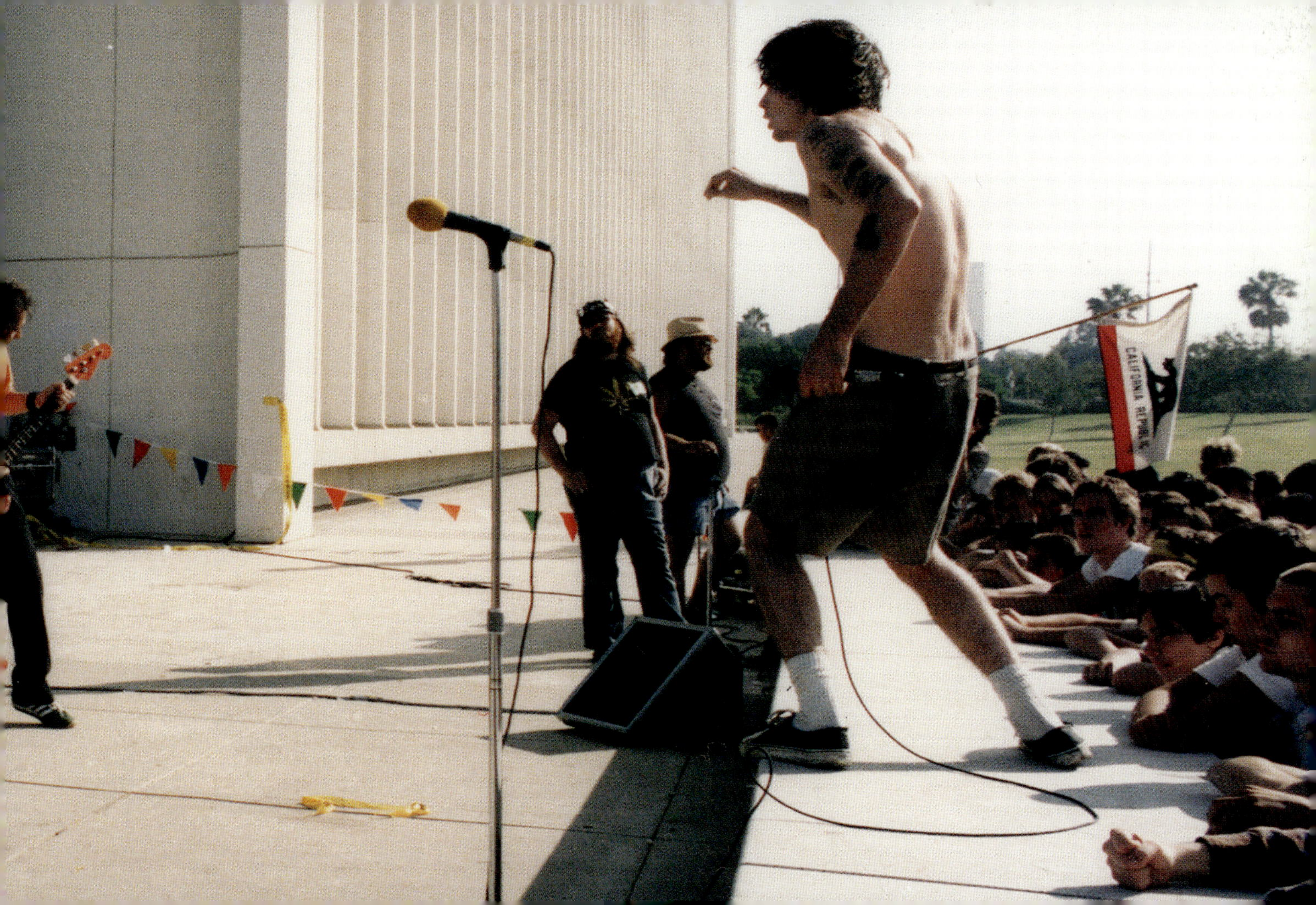
CALIFORNIA REPUBLIC

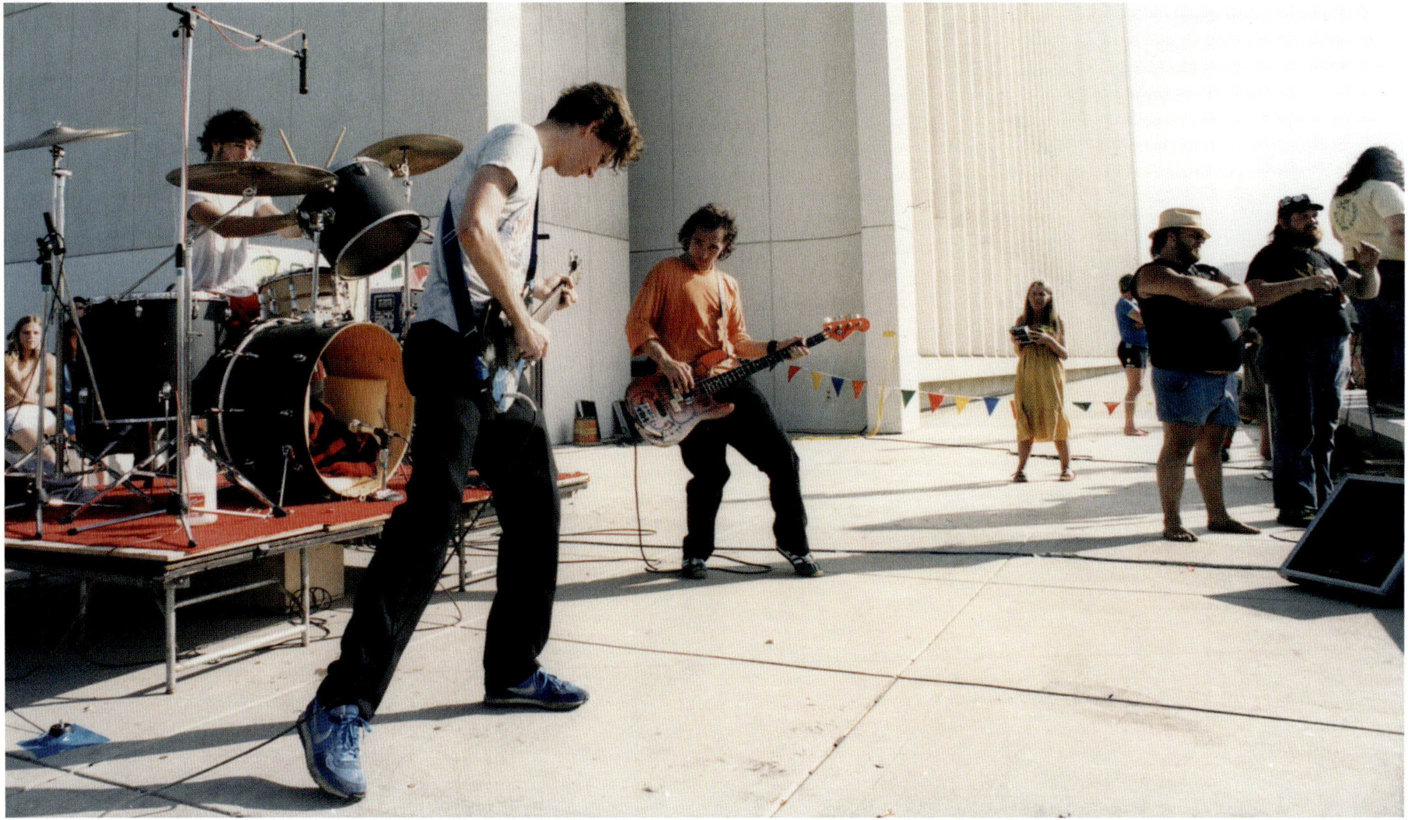

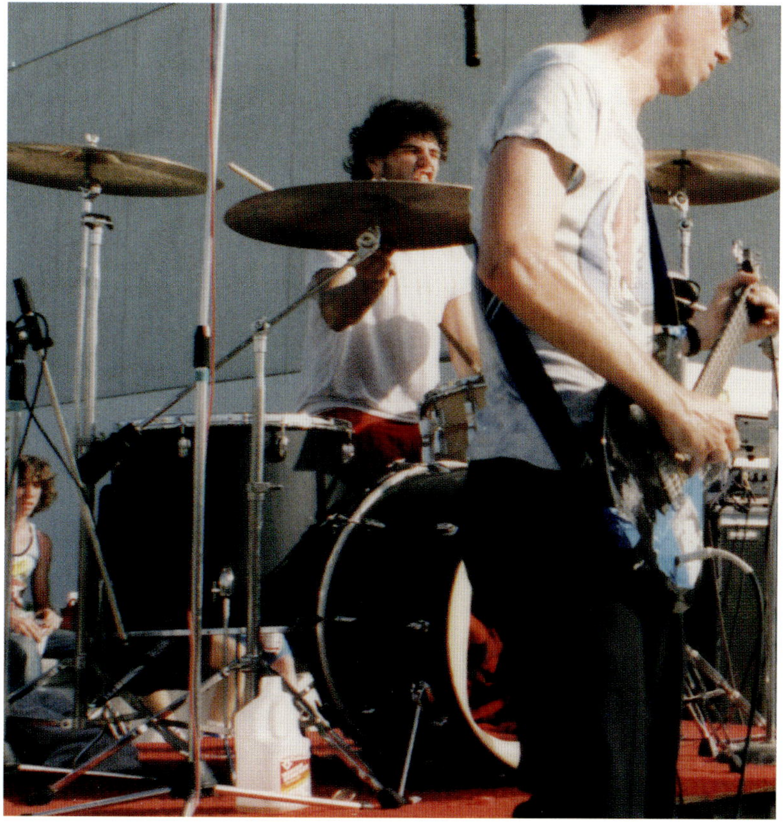

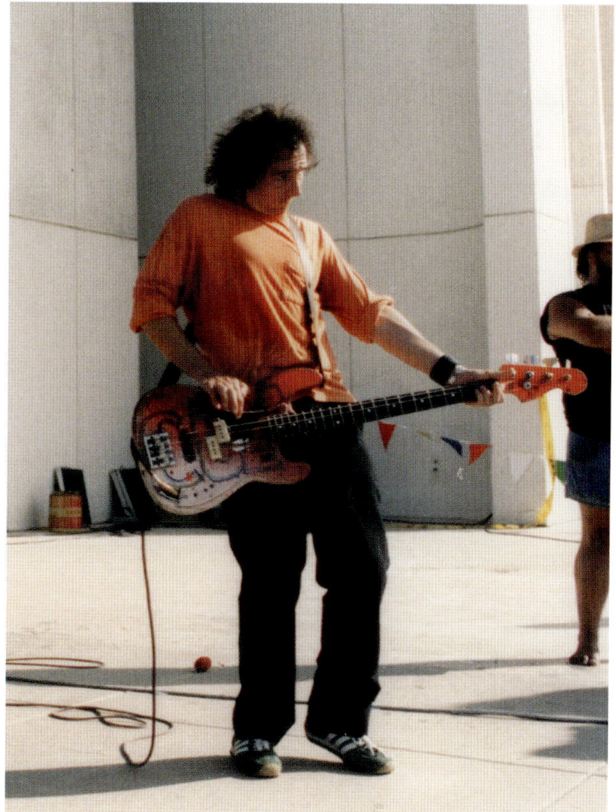

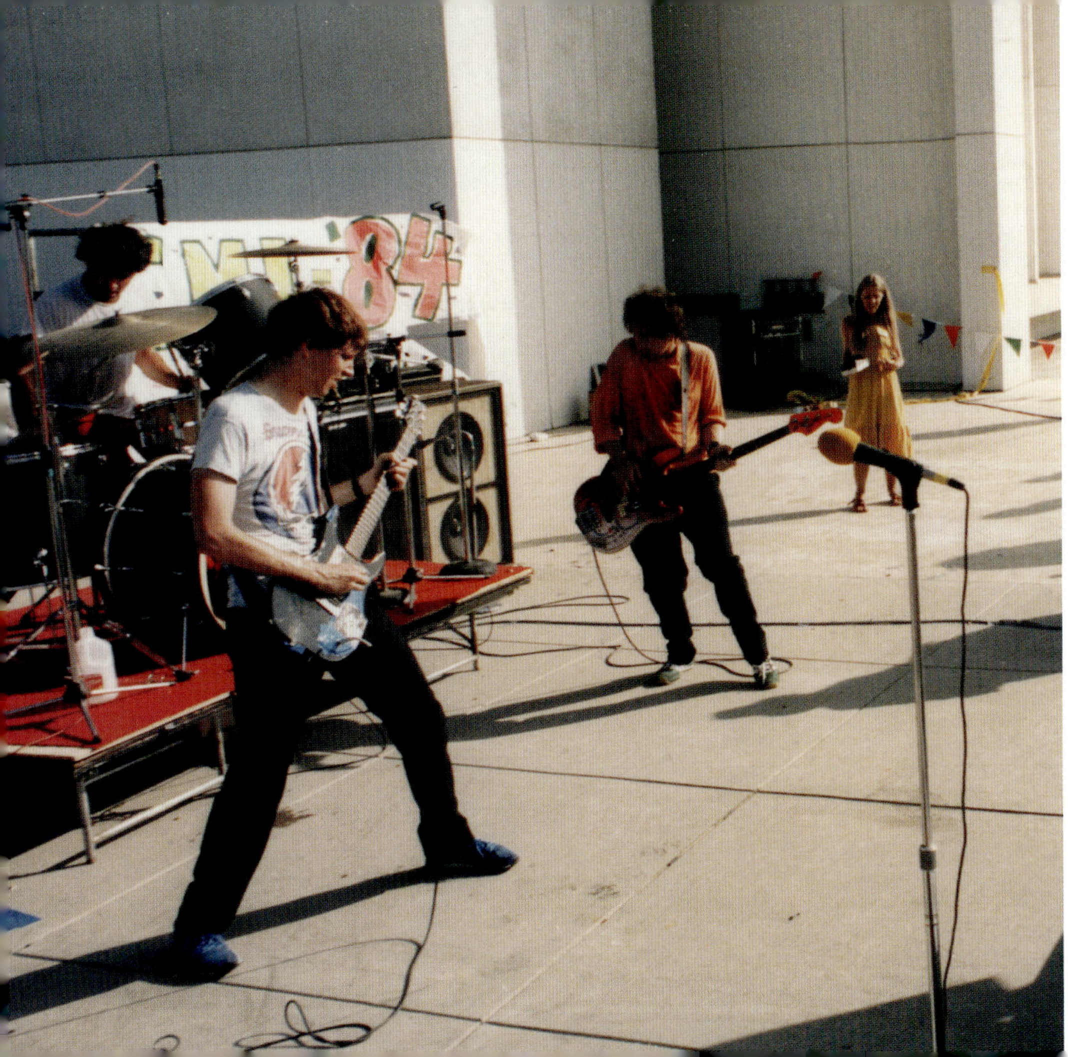

TENSION

People in the crowd recall helicopters passing overhead while Black Flag played. Others noticed FBI agents taking photos from inside and atop the roof of the Federal Building, and also from a field post set up at a nearby parking garage. No government documents of this event have yet surfaced, however.

An aura of menace surrounded Black Flag, and their movement were not loved by law enforcement.

"Yeah man, it's Independence Day, you've gotta respect it, like don't be too free!"
—Chuck Dukowski

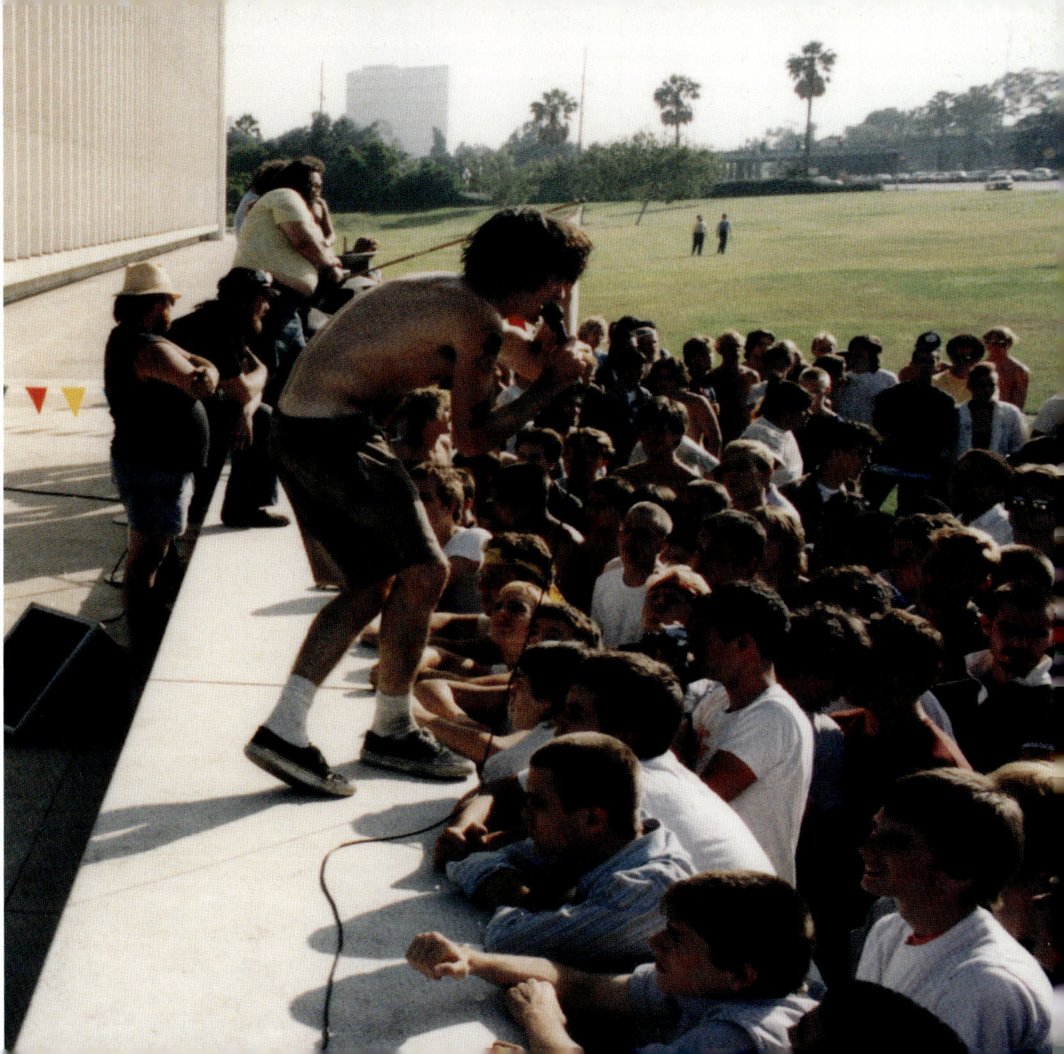

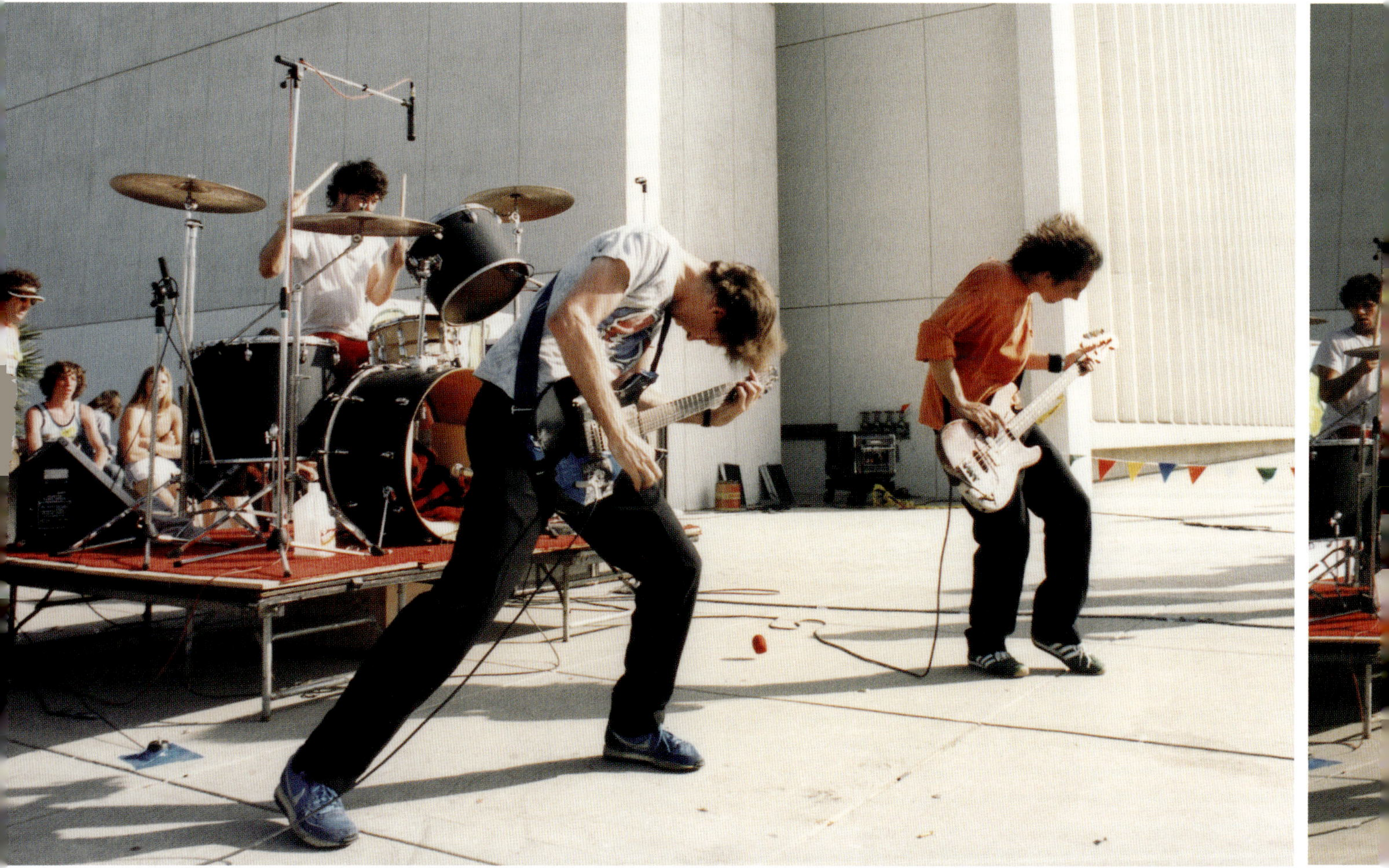

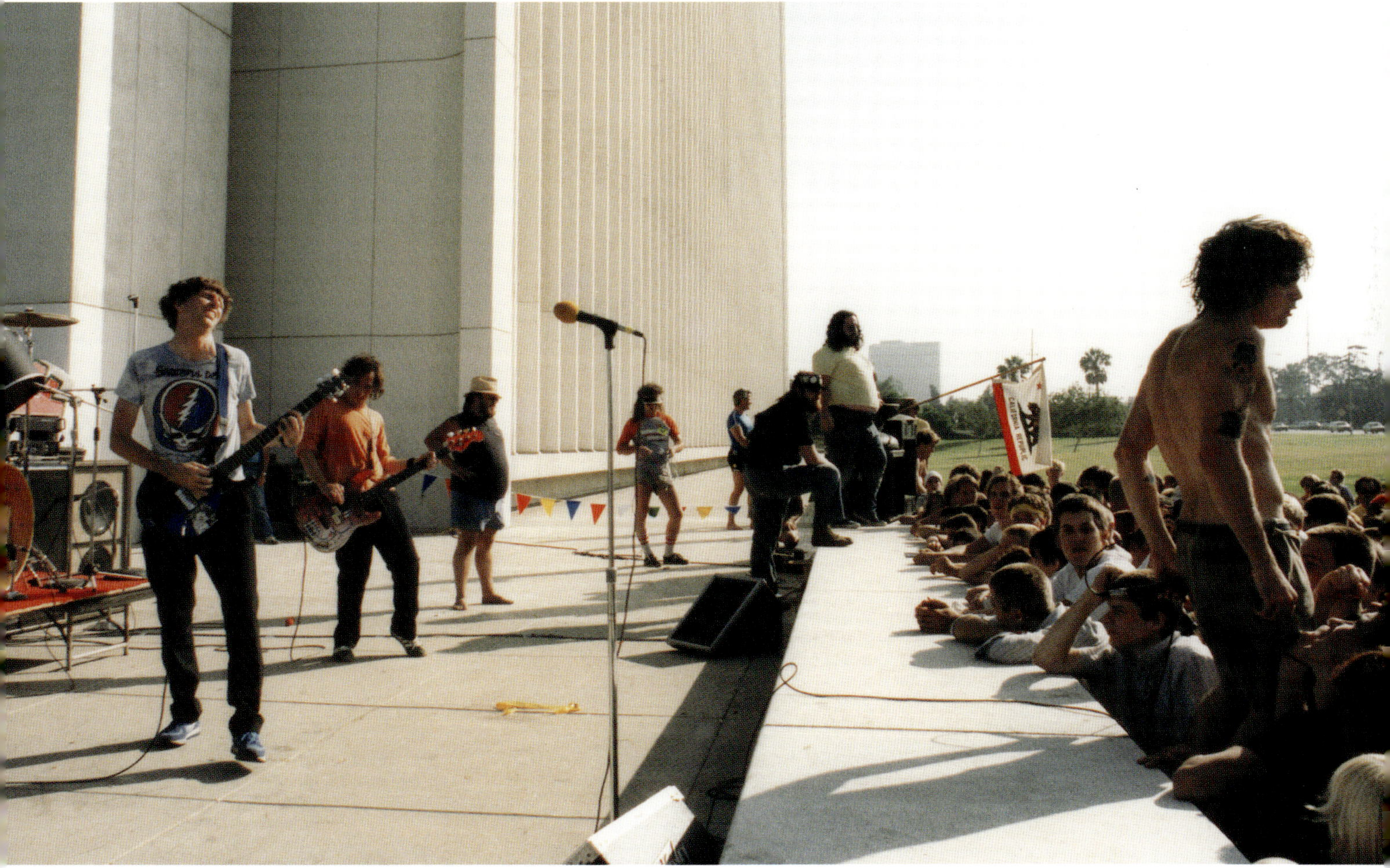

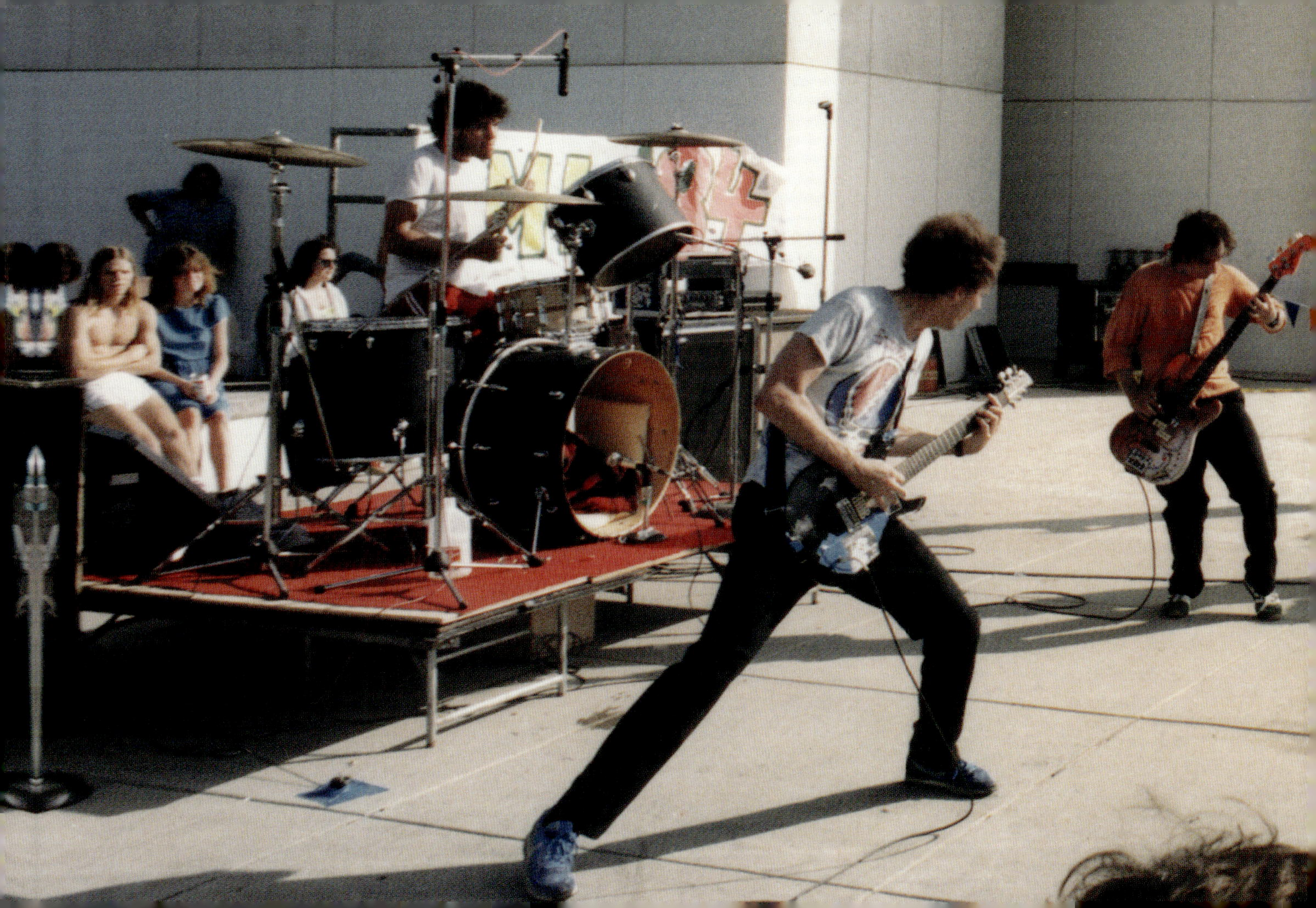

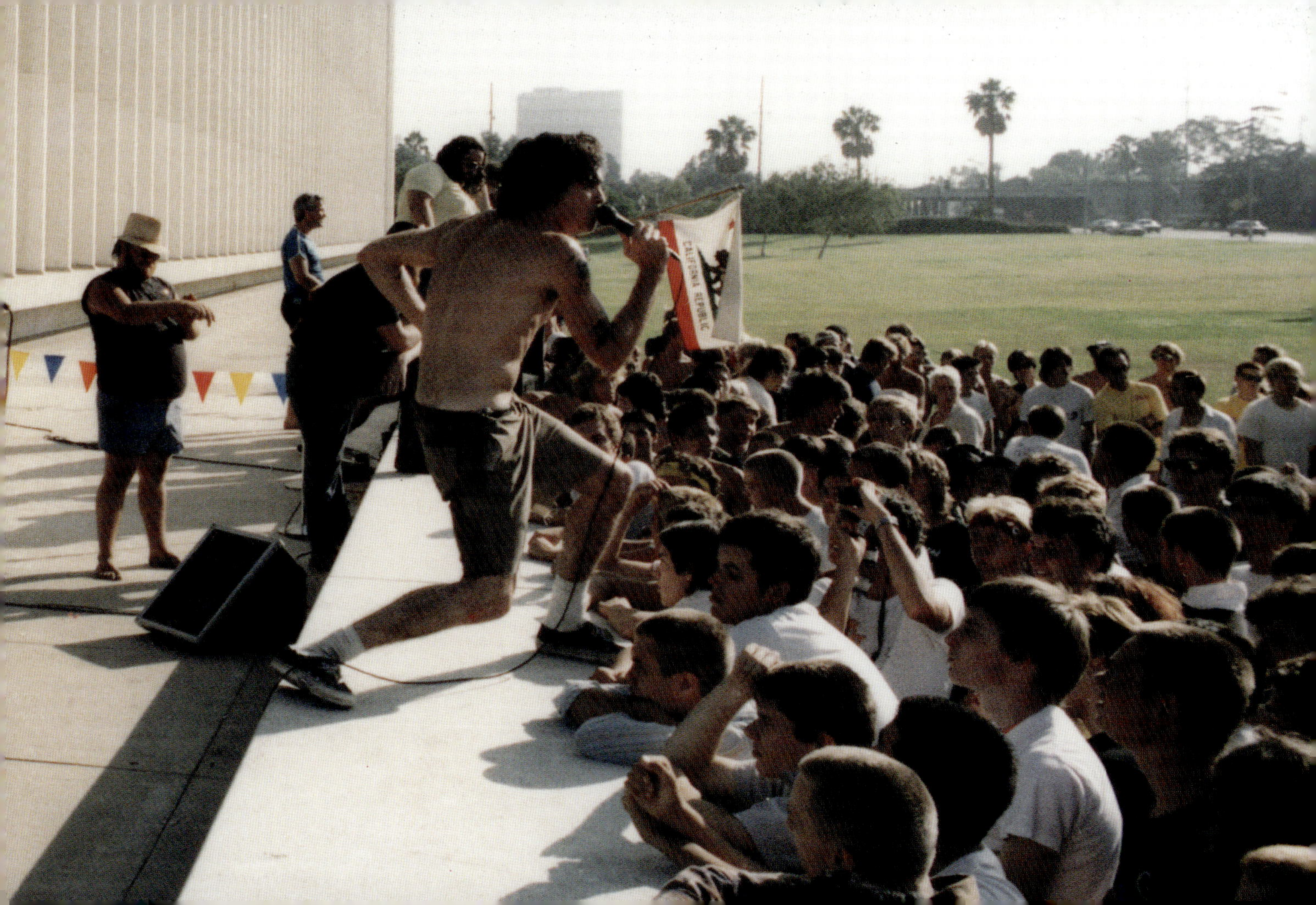
CALIFORNIA REPUBLIC

BLACK FLAG SUMMER

"During the summer of 1983, this version of Black Flag felt unstoppable. We saw them play everywhere we could. The shows that stick with me most are this surreal daytime set at the Federal Building, where punk collided with politics, and the volatile and energetic show at the Vex later that month—it felt like anything could happen at any moment. They were the same band, playing the same songs, but in completely different worlds. Seeing them in those settings completely inspired me."—David O. Jones, Alice Bag/the Deadbeats/Carnage Asada

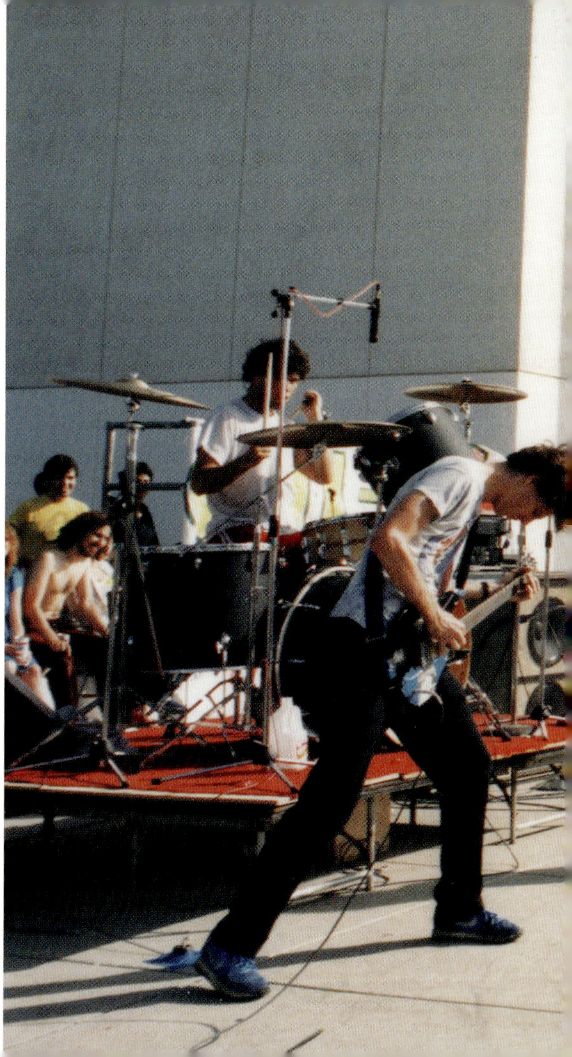

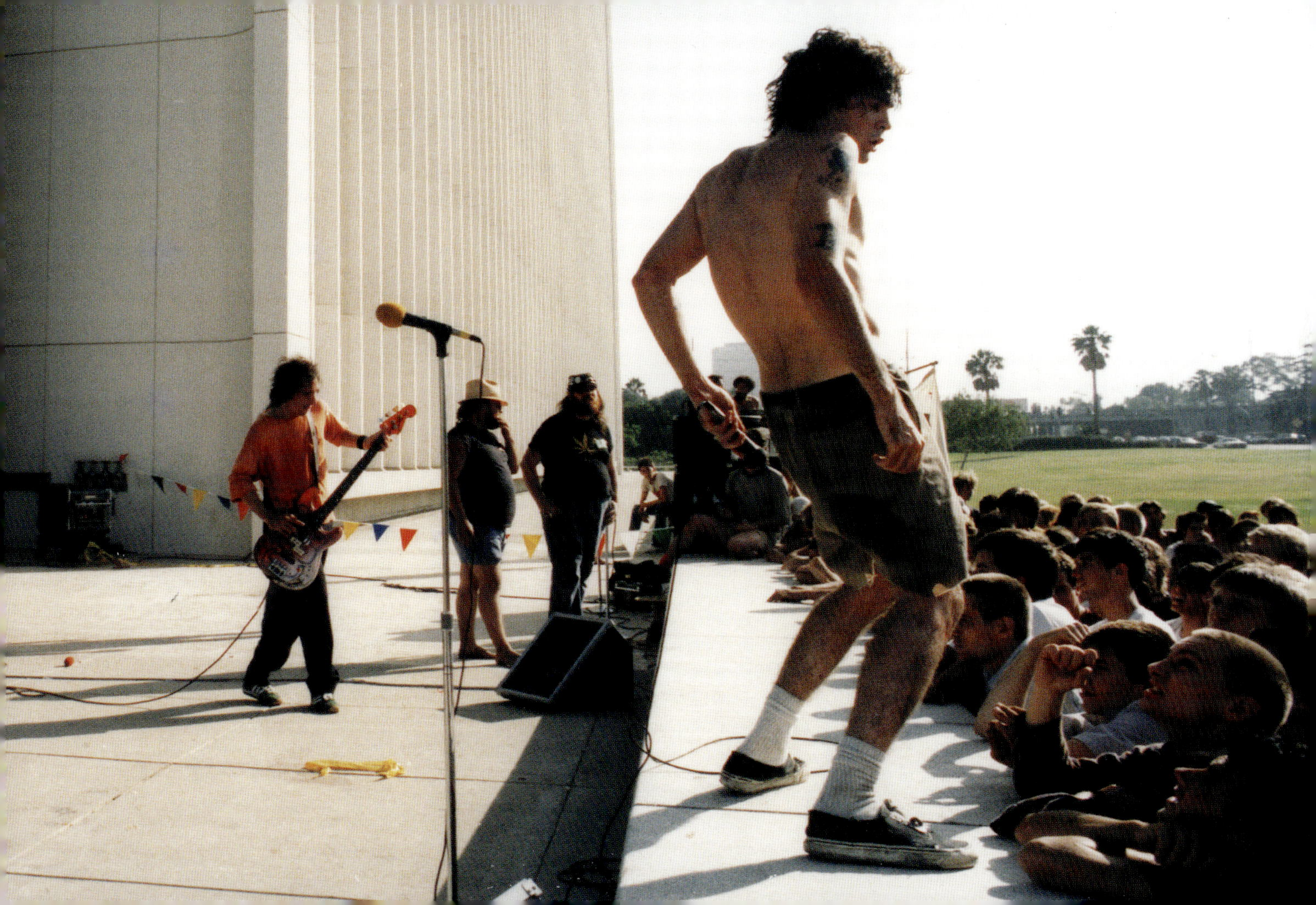

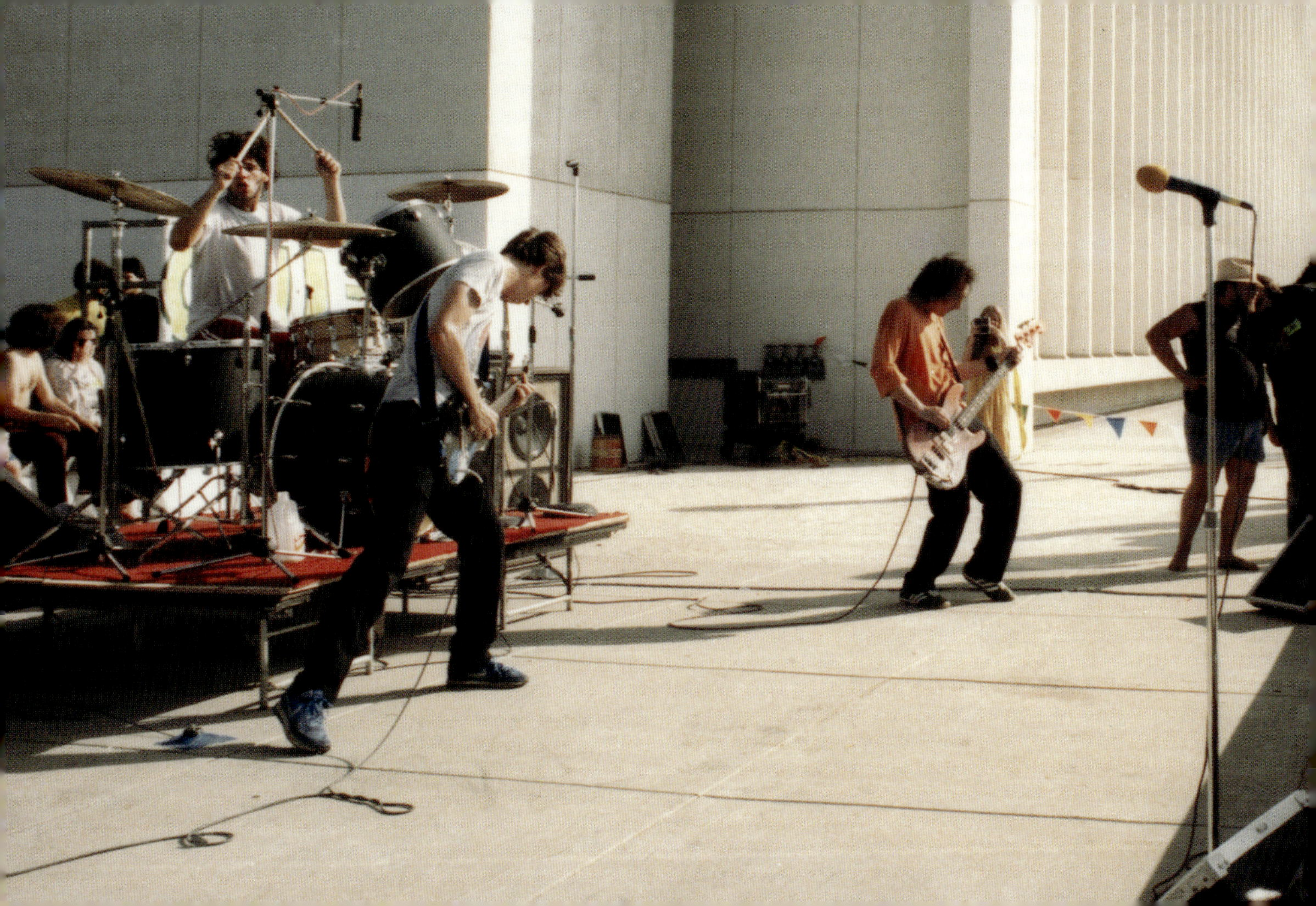

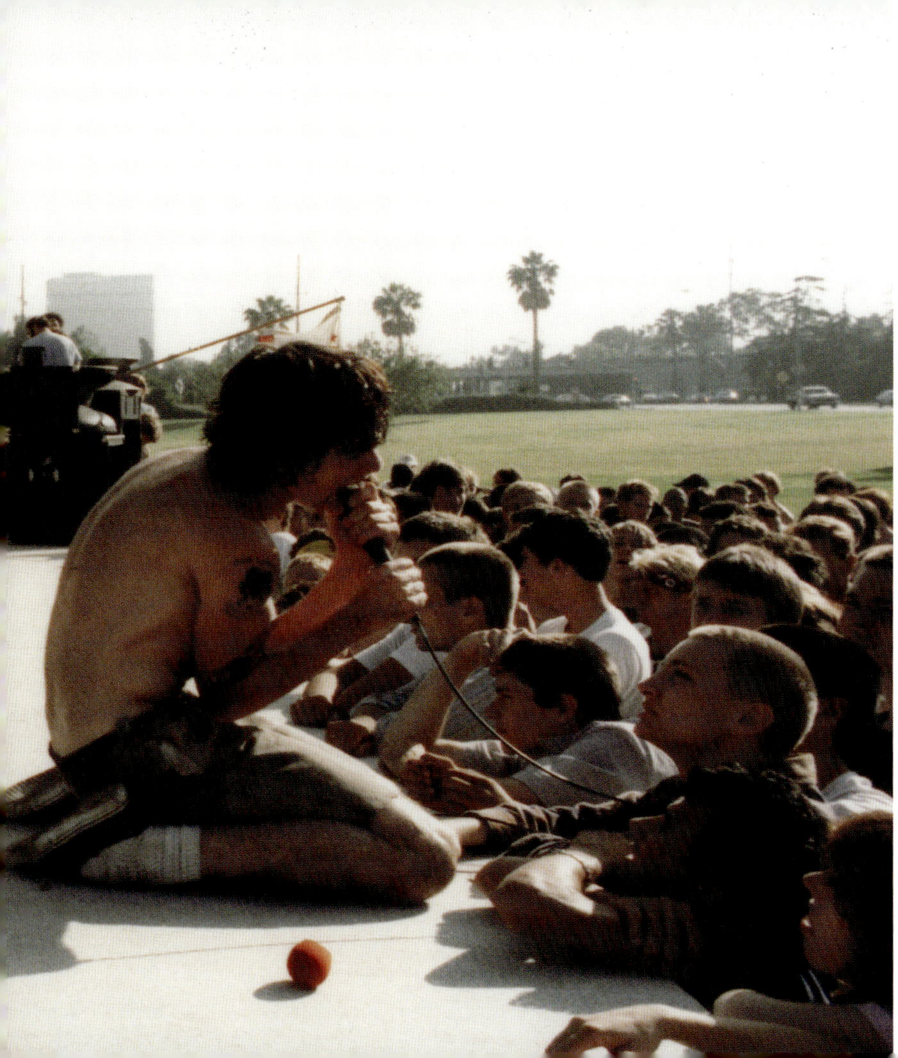

WILSHIRE FEDERAL BUILDING : JULY 4, 1983

Wasted

Slip It In

Can't Decide

Black Coffee

Nothing Left Inside

My War

Six Pack

Rise Above

Jealous Again

Louie Louie

Thirsty And Miserable

!!!!

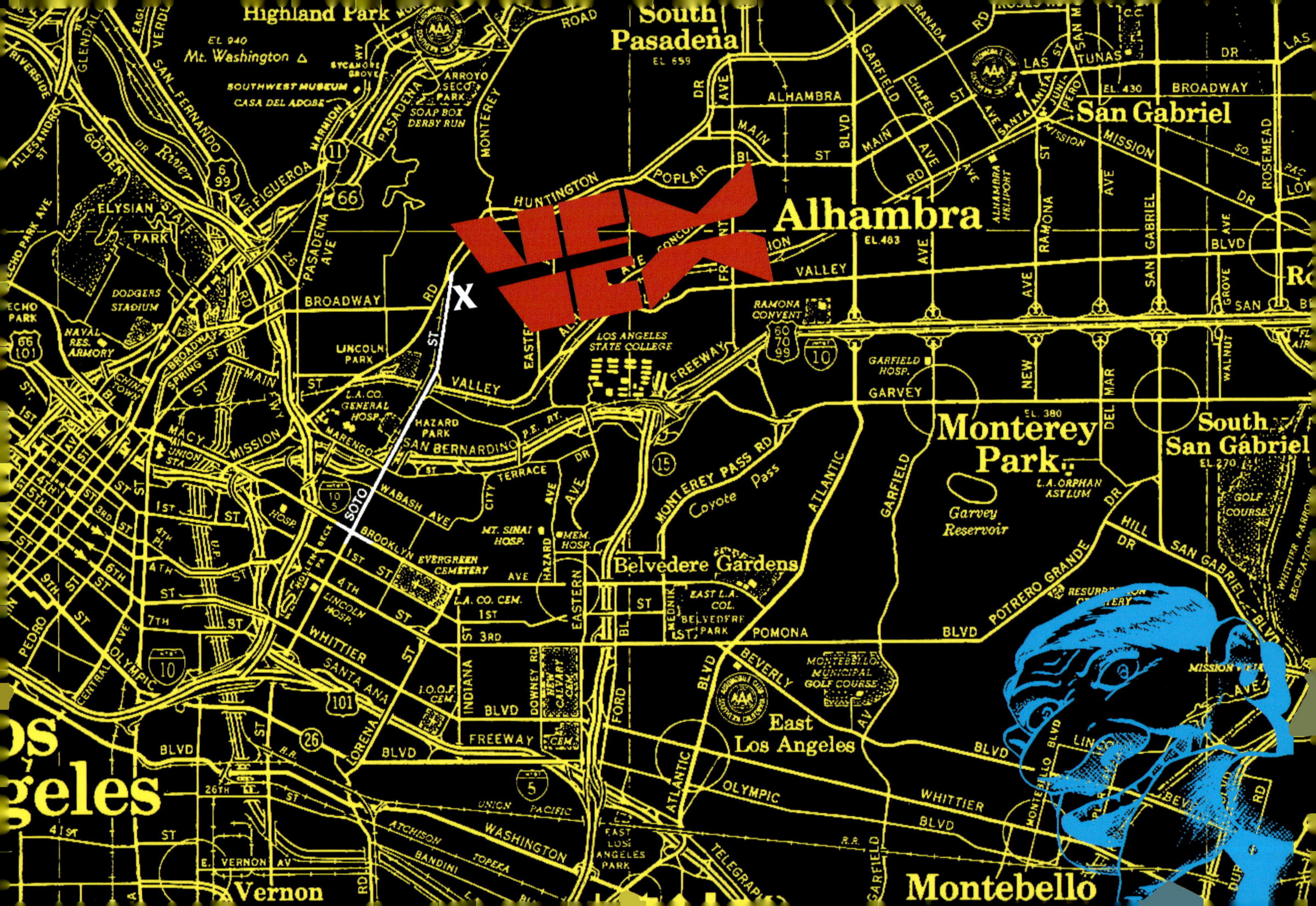

Highland Park
South Pasadena
EL 659
EL 940
Mt. Washington
SOUTHWEST MUSEUM
CASA DEL ADOBE
ARROYO SECO PARK
SOAP BOX DERBY RUN
San Gabriel
EL. 430
Alhambra
EL.483
ALHAMBRA HELIPORT
ELYSIAN STATE PARK
DODGERS STADIUM
ECHO PARK
NAVAL RES. ARMORY
LINCOLN PARK
L.A. CO. GENERAL HOSP.
HAZARD PARK
RAMONA CONVENT
LOS ANGELES STATE COLLEGE
GARFIELD HOSP.
Monterey Park
EL. 380
South San Gabriel
EL.270
L.A. ORPHAN ASYLUM
Garvey Reservoir
Coyote Pass
MONTEREY PASS RD
MT. SINAI HOSP.
MEM. HOSP.
EVERGREEN CEMETERY
LINCOLN HOSP.
L.A. CO. CEM.
Belvedere Gardens
EAST L.A. COL.
BELVEDERE PARK
MONTEBELLO MUNICIPAL GOLF COURSE
RESURRECTION CEMETERY
I.O.O.F. CEM.
NEW CALVARY CEM.
East Los Angeles
EAST LOS ANGELES PARK
Montebello
Vernon
Los Angeles
SOTO ST
X

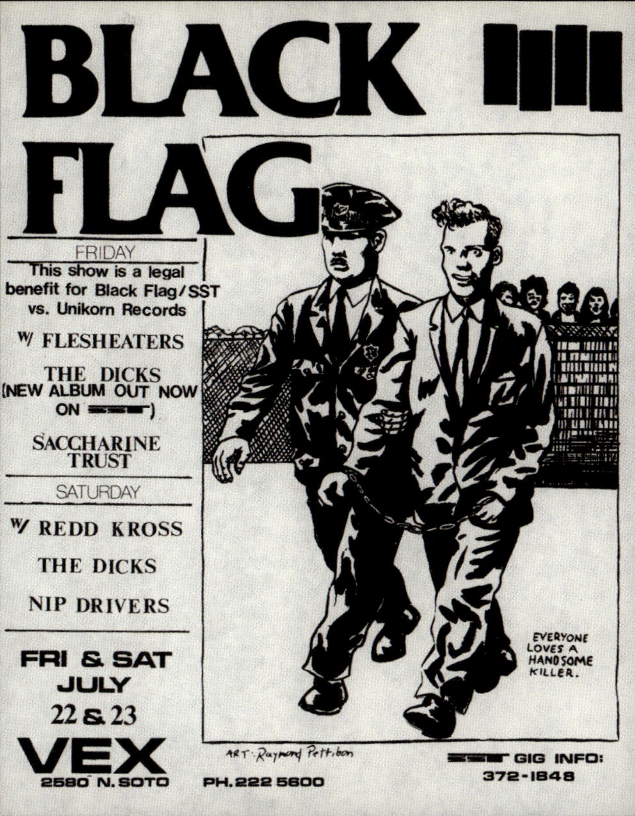

The Vex
2580 N. Soto
July 23, 1983

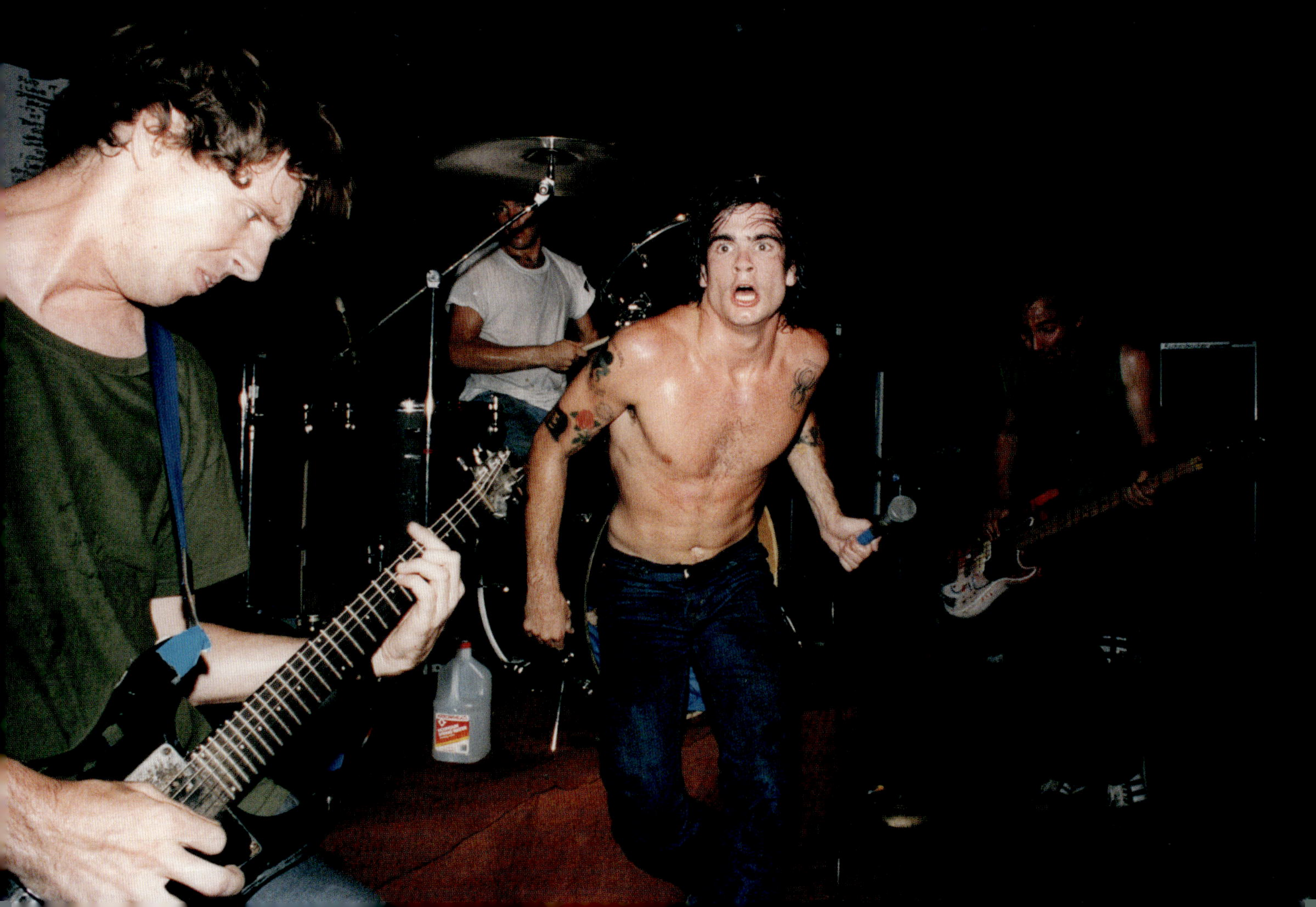

“NOTHING LEFT INSIDE”

Black Flag at the Vex took place on July 23, 1983. The flyer for the show says they would be joined by Redd Kross, the Dicks, and Nip Drivers, but they actually played with Redd Kross—who I missed—and Saint Vitus.

The summer of ‘83 was a turning point for Black Flag and for punk rock. A hard rock and metal kind of a pre-grunge sound was coming in, pioneered by Black Flag, Suicidal Tendencies, Discharge, Melvins, D.R.I., and a few other bands. Punks were beginning to grow out their hair, and there was a crossover with metal coming. New bands in L.A. like Slayer and Metallica were influenced by punk, unlike metal bands before them who thought “punk was bunk.”

Meanwhile, within Black Flag, Chuck Dukowski was being pushed out of the band by Greg Ginn. Black Flag’s music started to fragment into more experimental stuff. Then they released instrumental and spoken word albums. A friend of mine would go and hang out with Black Flag in Redondo Beach at Ginn’s SST Records’ unassuming headquarters/shop off Artesia Blvd. He reported back that there was tension between band members, and that Greg was often in a weird, unfriendly mood

In my opinion, this was the end of powerhouse Black Flag as we knew it. Chuck Dukowski to me was the heart of the band. He brought so much power and intensity. Kira Roessler was an excellent bass player, but nobody had the power or propulsive energy that Chuck had. He had written, or cowritten, many of their great songs: "I've Heard it Before," "American Waste," "My War," and "Padded Cell."

Unfortunately, by the time the songs were recorded for the *My War* album in December 1984, they had lost some power, as well as a feeling of chaos and danger. The production was weaker, and Ginn played the bass instead of Dukowski. Ginn played technically correctly, but without the heart and soul of Chuck. Black Flag would never be the same.

Chuck played his last show with Black Flag on August 5, two weeks after these Vex photos. This was pretty much the end of the road as we knew it. Soon after, Black Flag would lose its deep unbelievable intensity. As much as Henry gave his all, things wouldn't be the same.

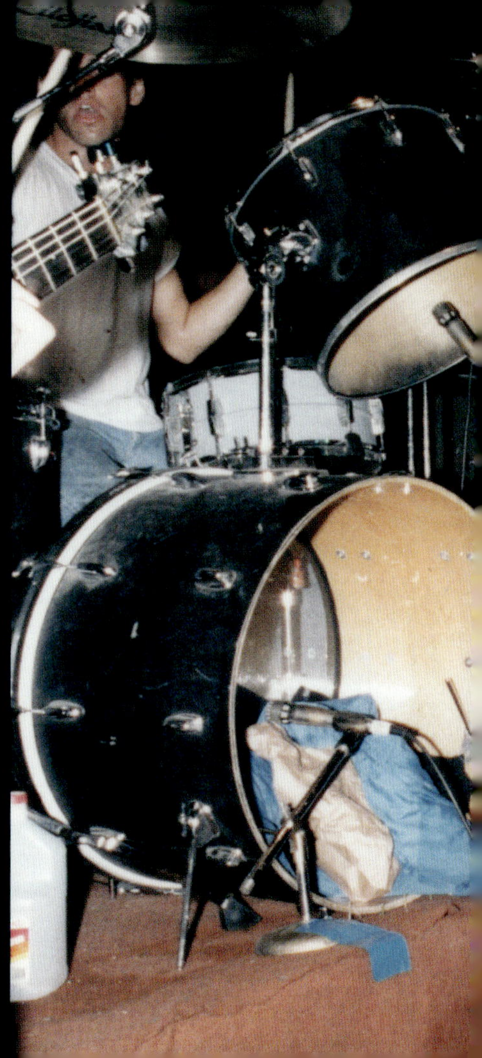

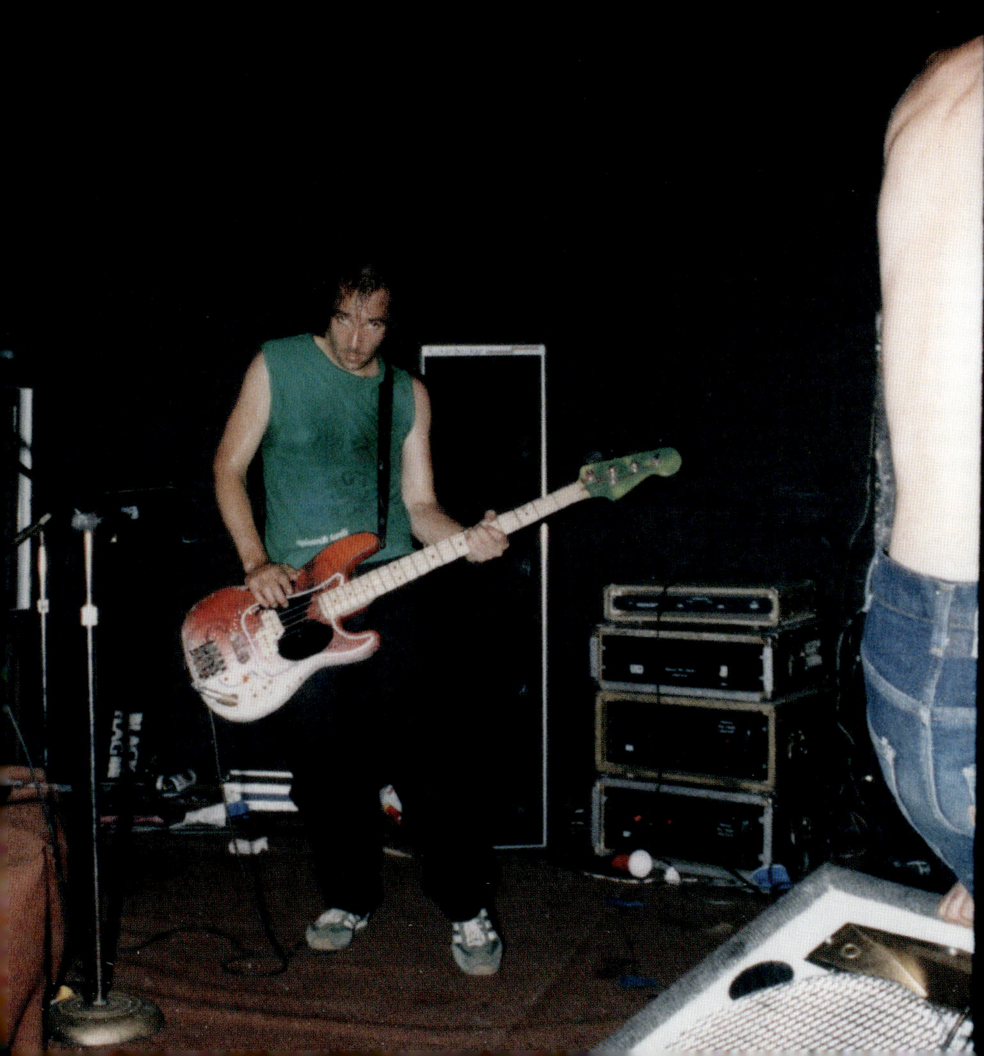

SAINT VITUS

Dave Chandler - guitar

Mark Adams - bass

Armando Acosta - drums

Scott Reagers - vocals

The band began opening for Black Flag in late 1982, They went on to release several albums on Greg Ginn's SST Records, beginning with their self-titled debut in 1984.

"We hooked up with Black Flag and started doing our first punk shows around 1982. They didn't mess around. The punks *hated* us for about three years. We called those days "the Punk Wars." By 1986, they kind of liked us, or at least respected us for never backing down. We only did punk shows, no metal—the metal scene always hated us, always. Those early days are my favorite times in Saint Vitus."—Dave Chandler

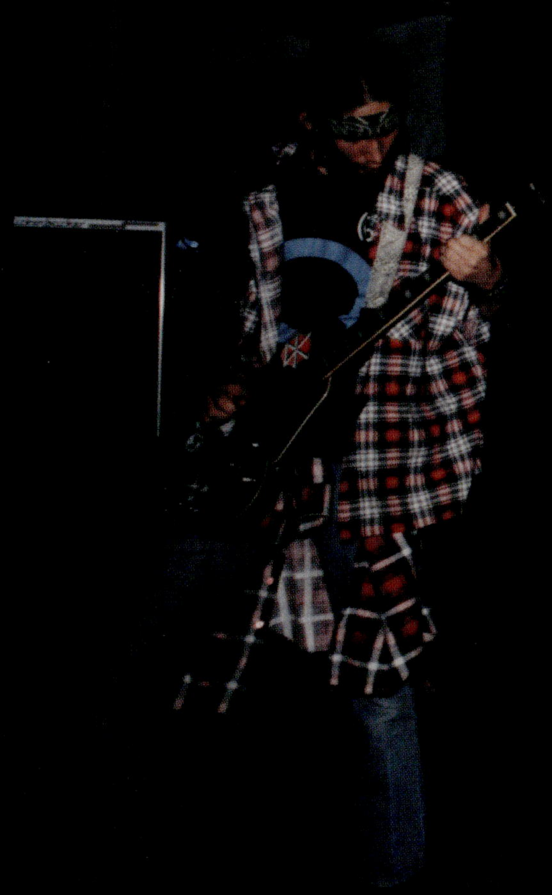

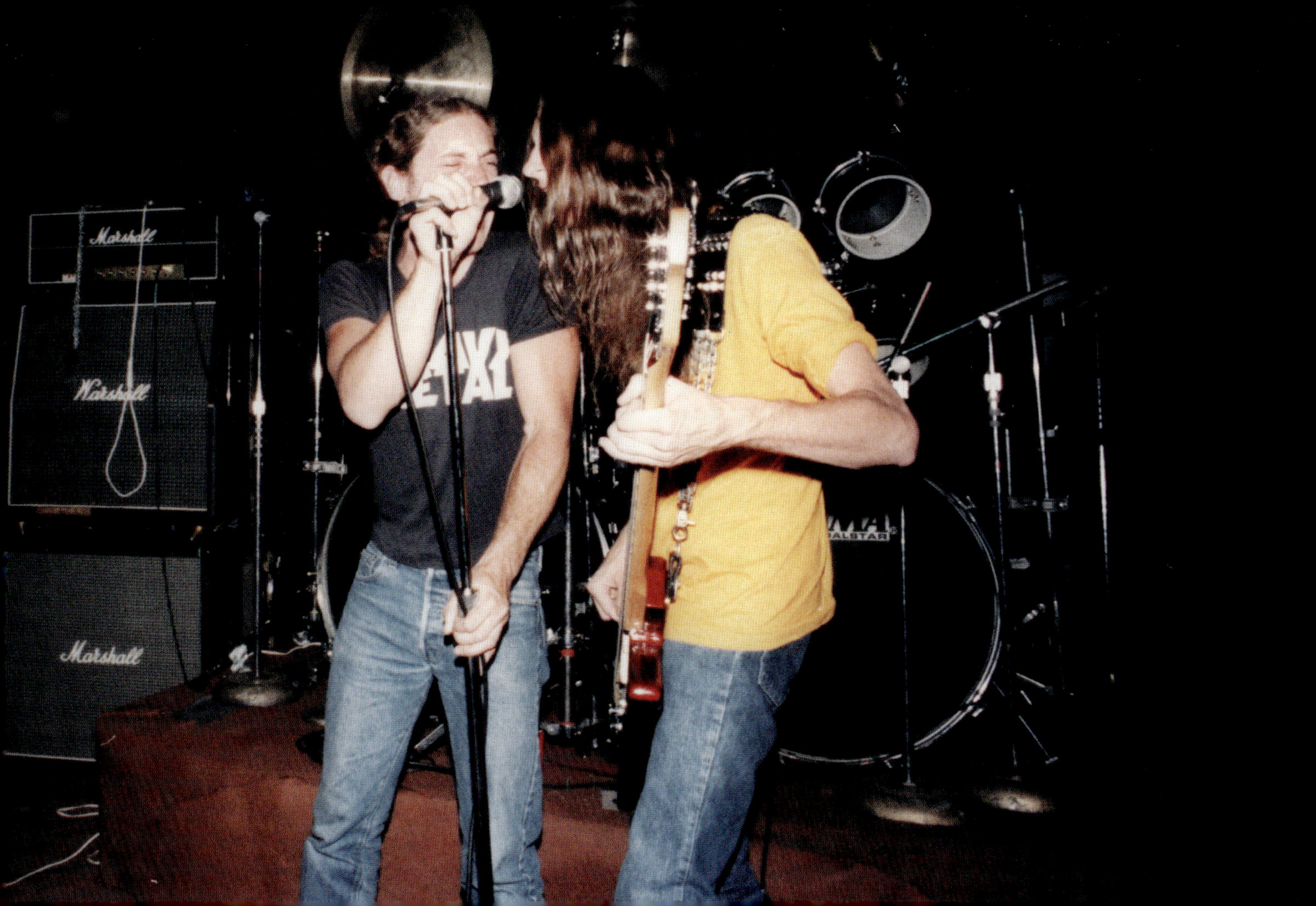
Marshall
Marshall
Marshall

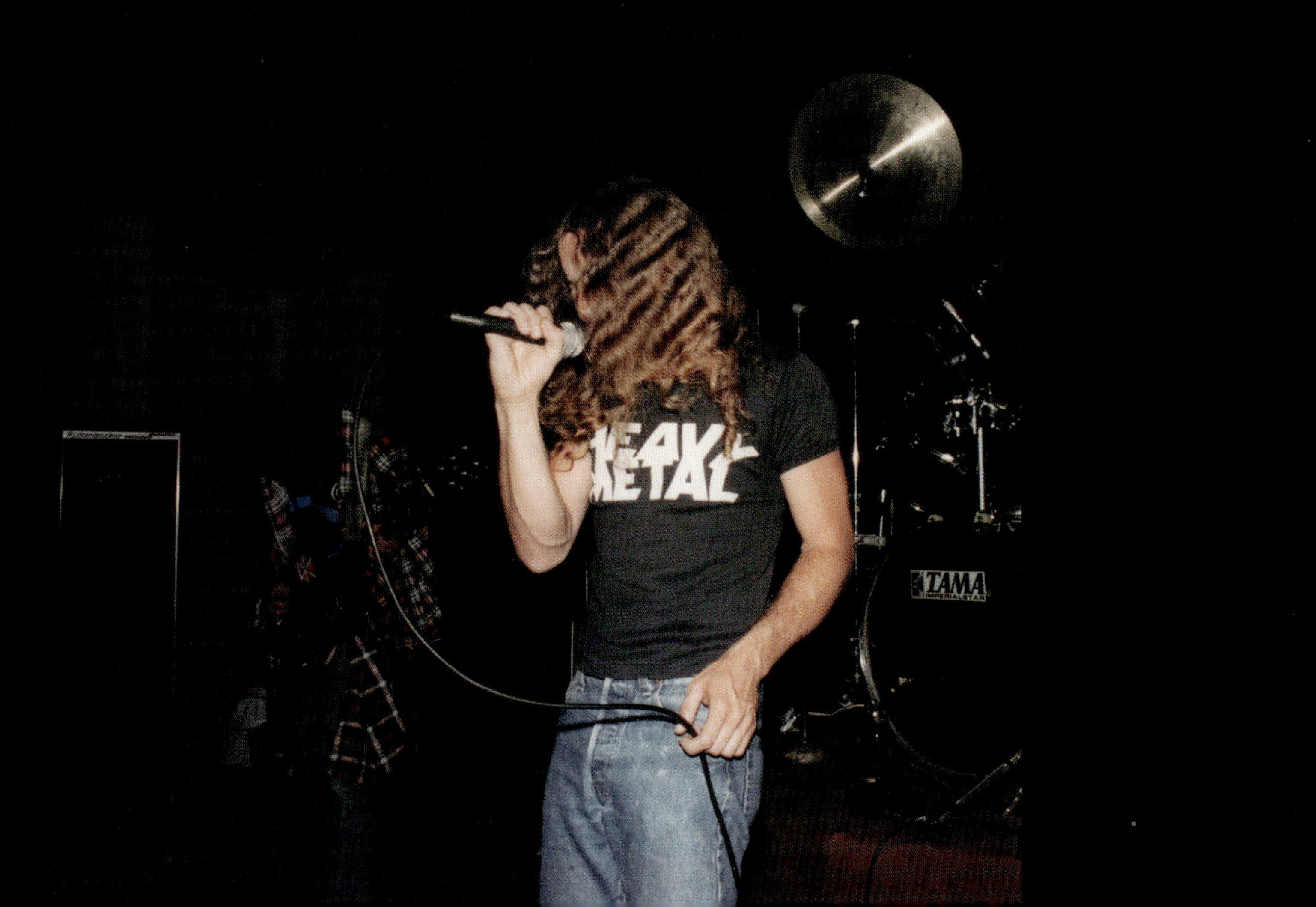
TAMA

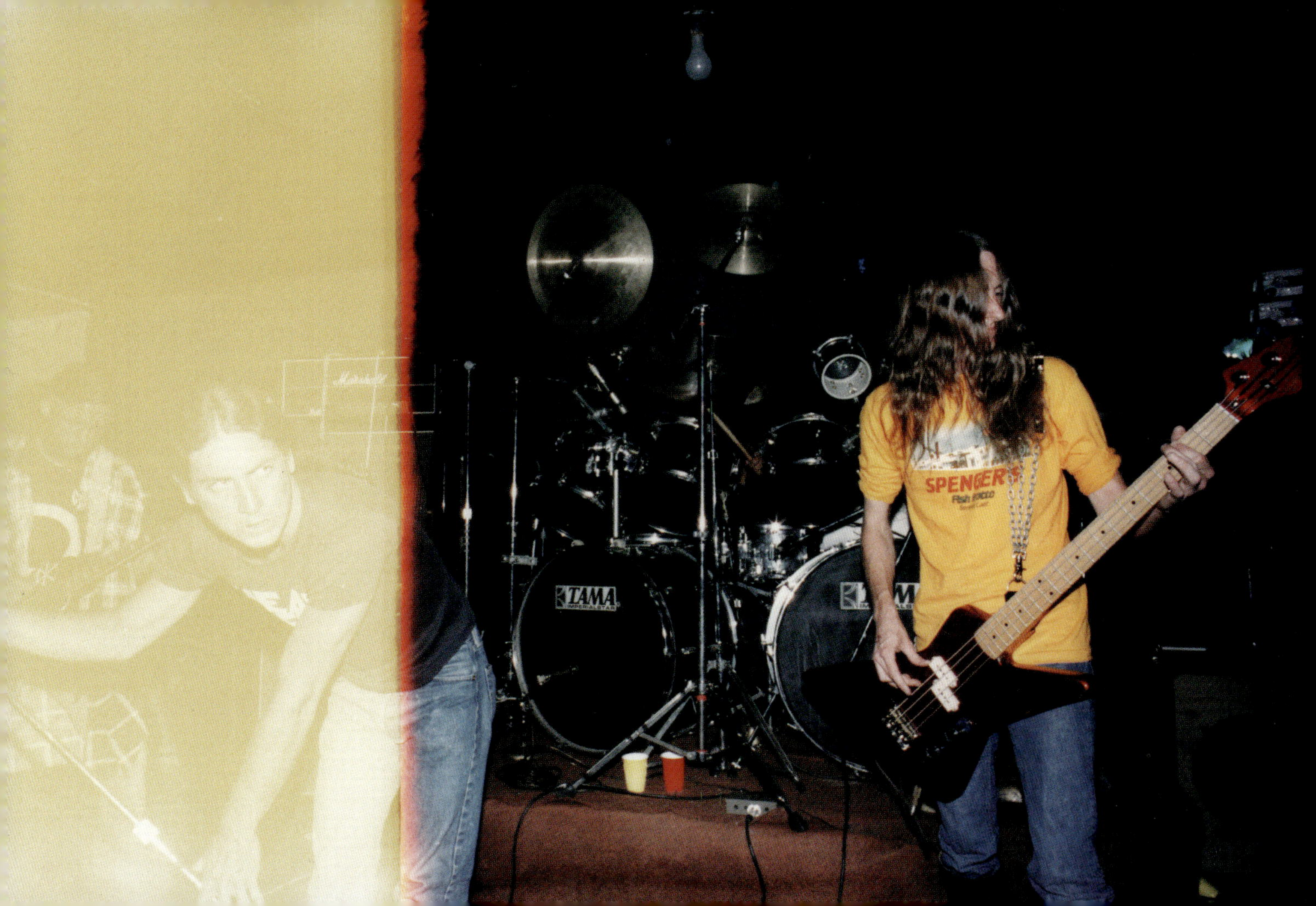
SPENGER'S
TAMA
IMPERIALSTAR

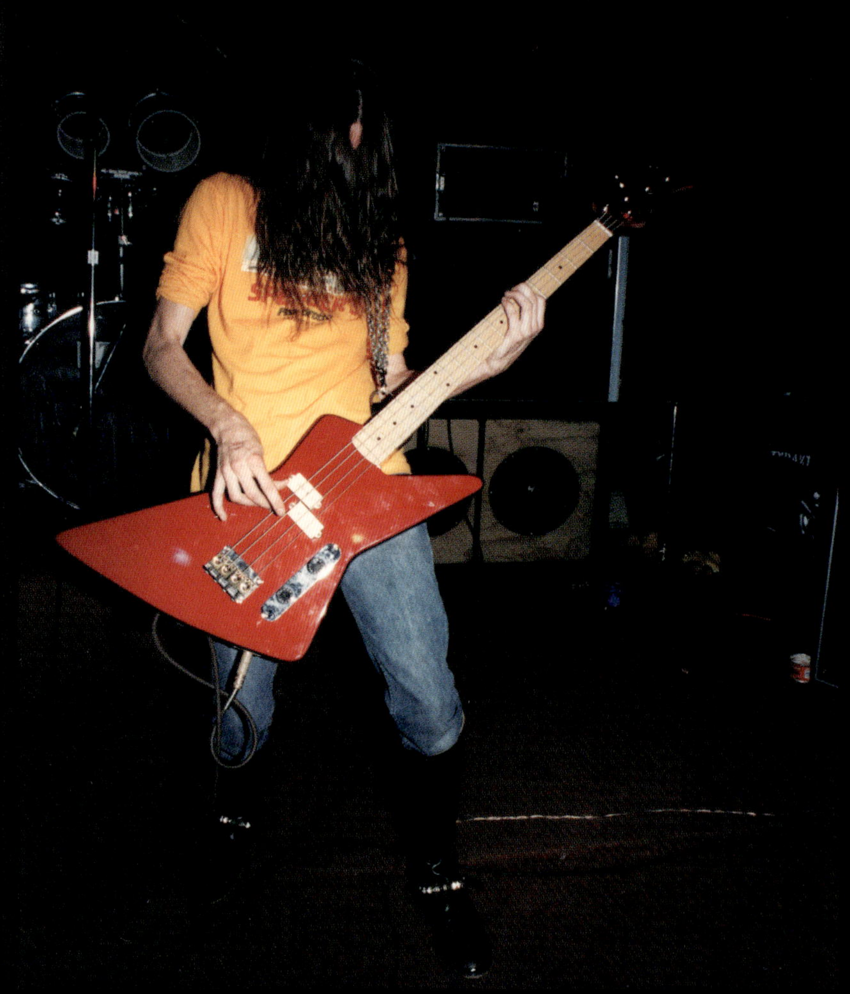

VITUS AT THE VEX

"The Vex used to have a permanent location. By the time we were doing his shows, though, the promoter, Joe Vex, had a different place every time. The show would go until the cops or whoever shut it down, then the next one would be somewhere else. We played the Vex three times in three different locations, one of them with Black Flag. Those were crazy times."
—Dave Chandler, Saint Vitus

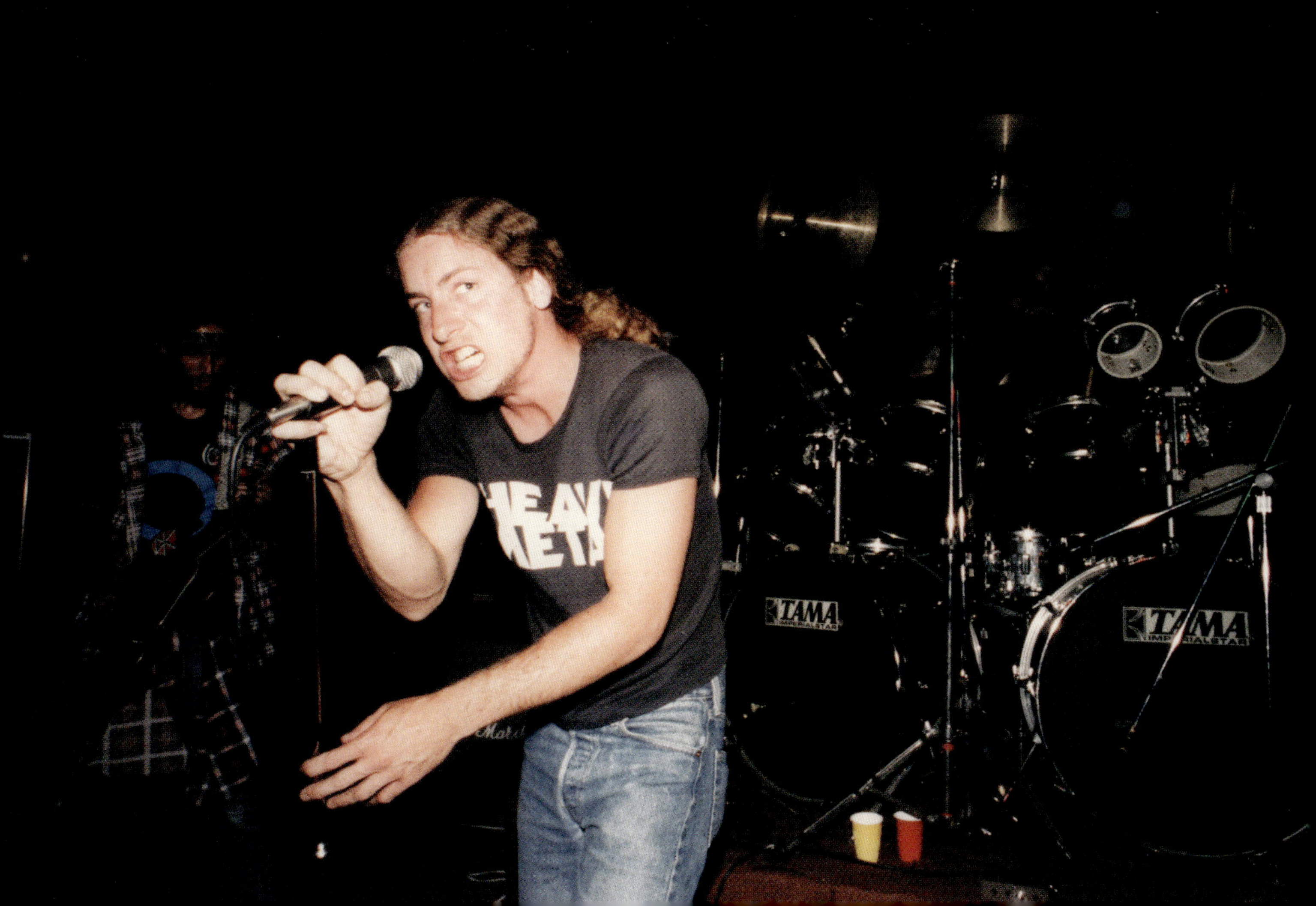
TAMA
TAMA
IMPERIALSTAR

THE VEX

"We played two nights at a club called The Vex. The club was located in a bad part of town. When we got to the gig there was local guys hired as security. They were carrying guns around the parking lot and people were getting pretty freaked out. When people walked in the front door they were searched. The girls got searched extra carefully,

—Henry Rollins, *GET IN THE VAN*

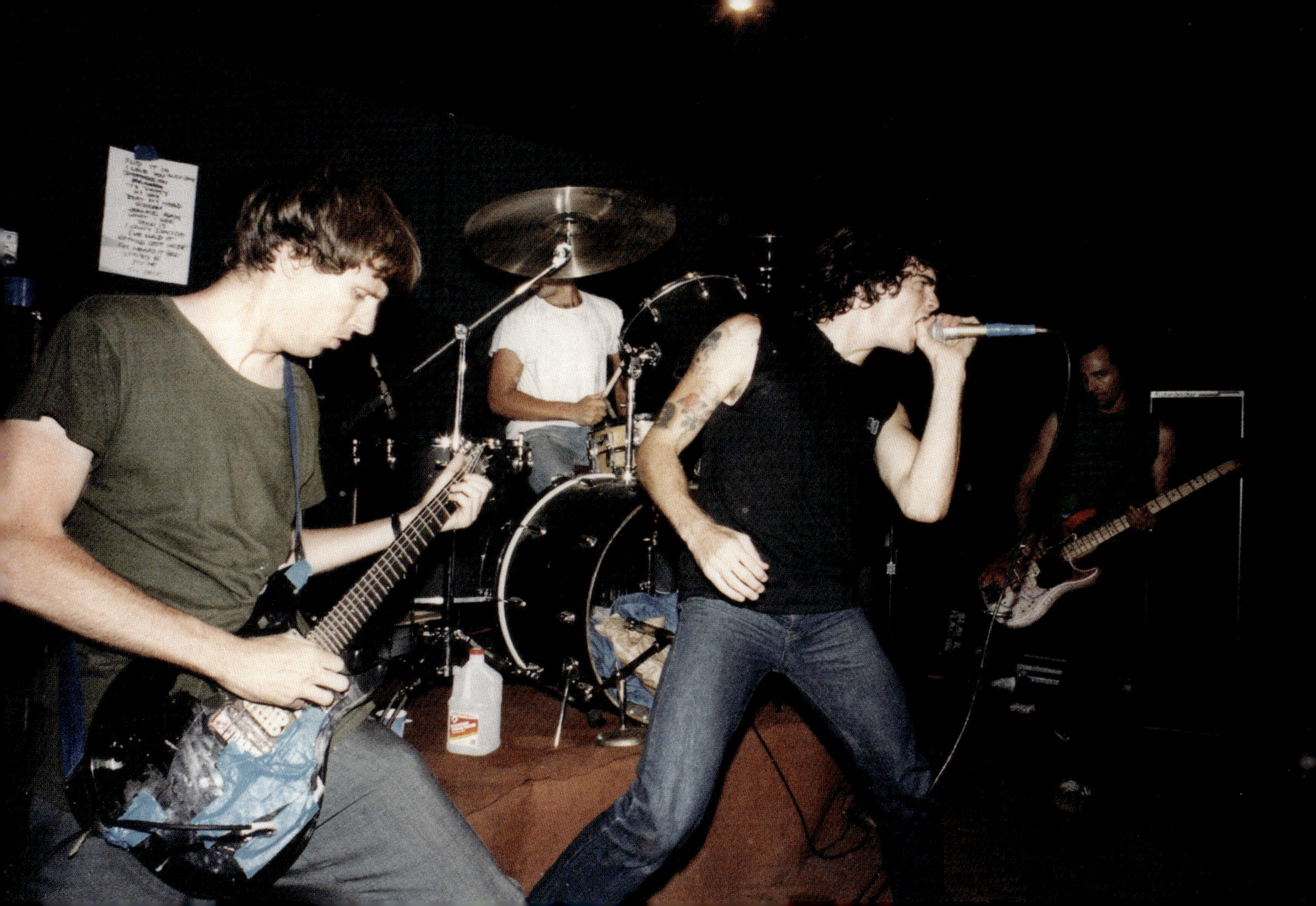

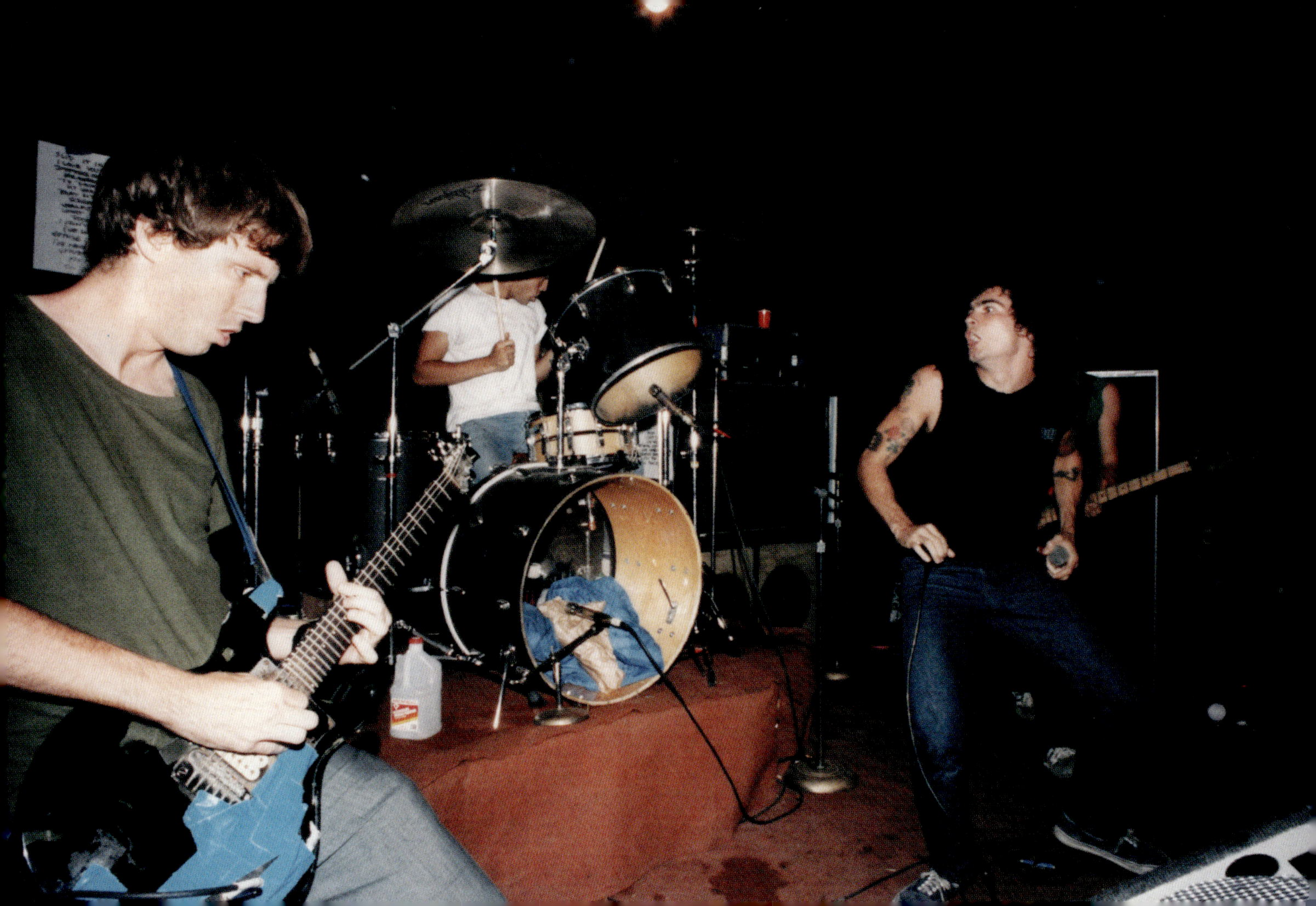

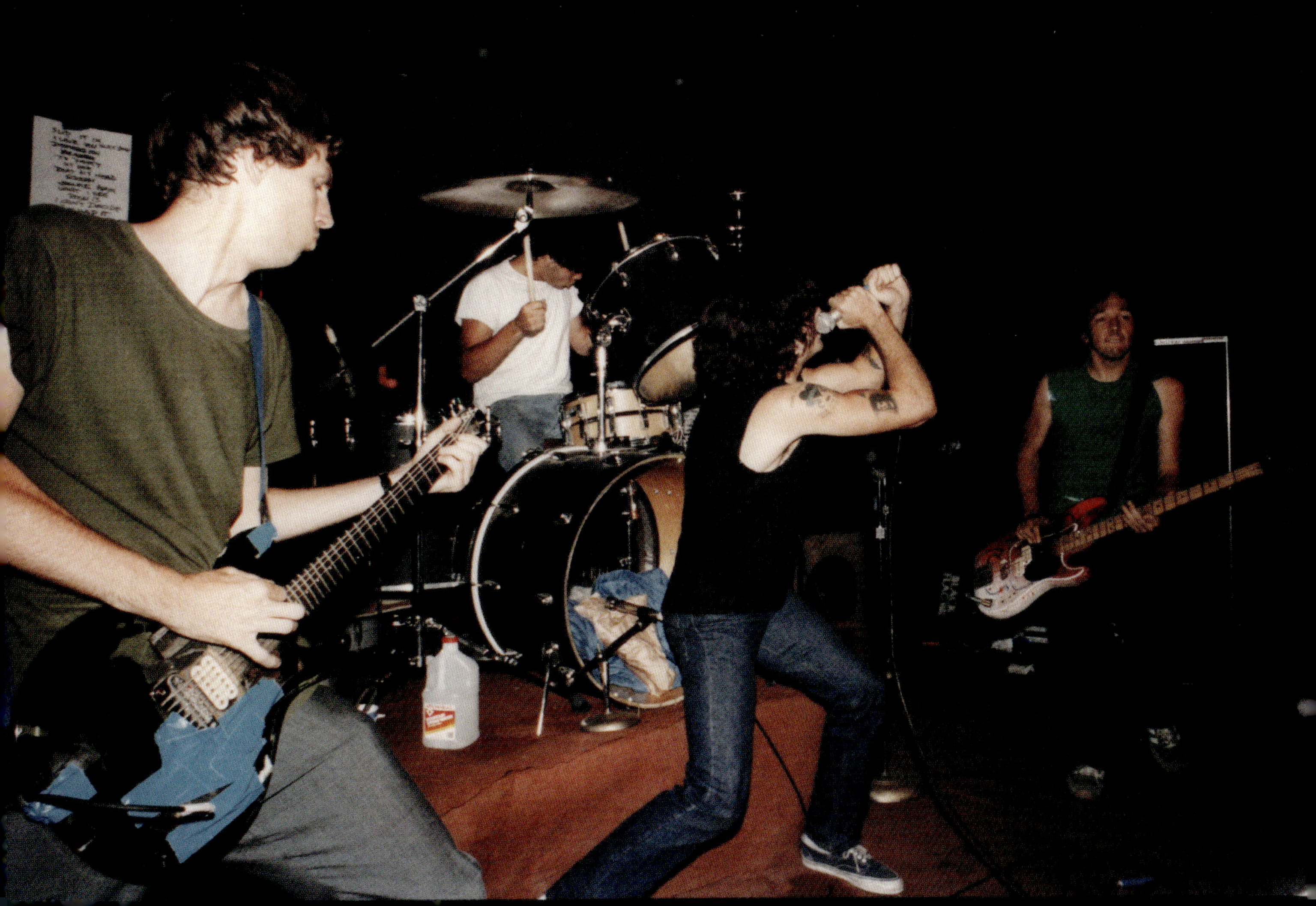

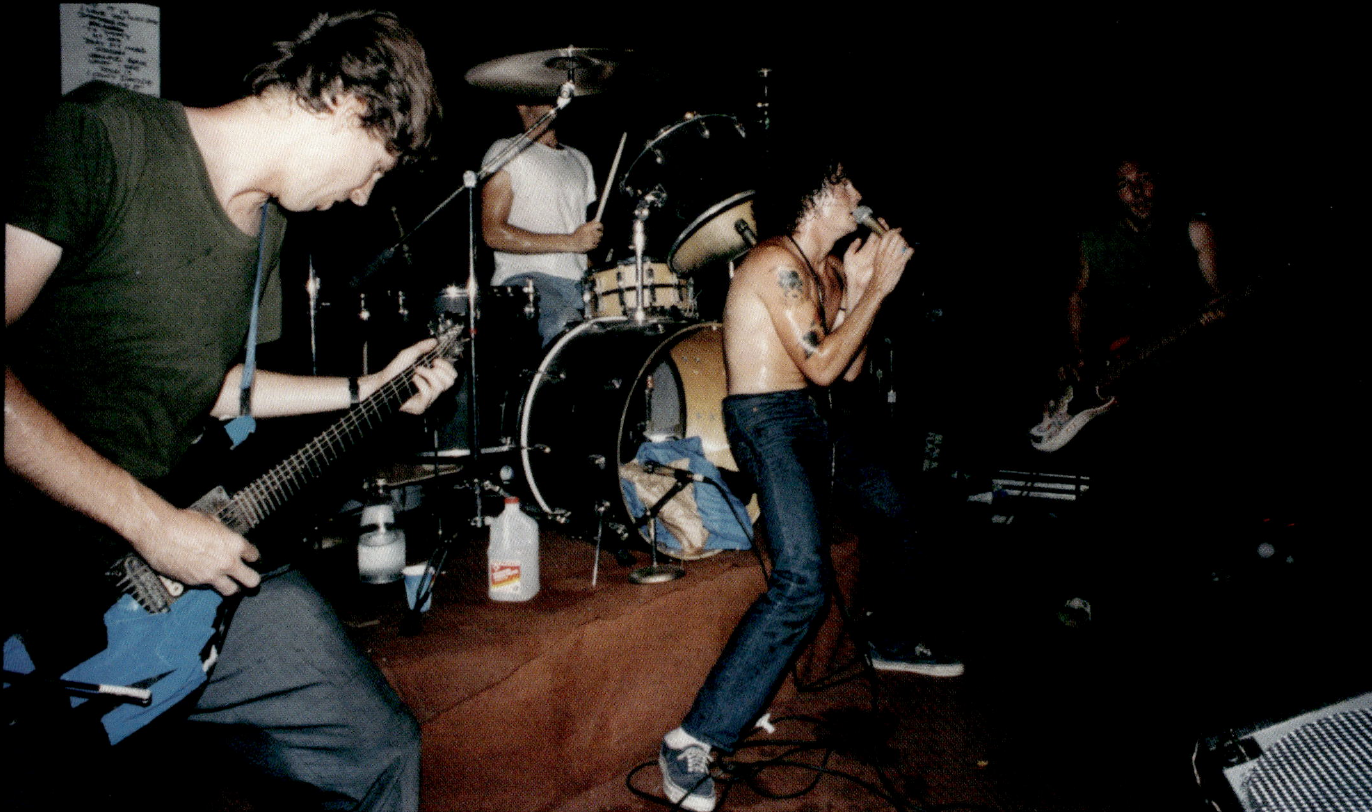

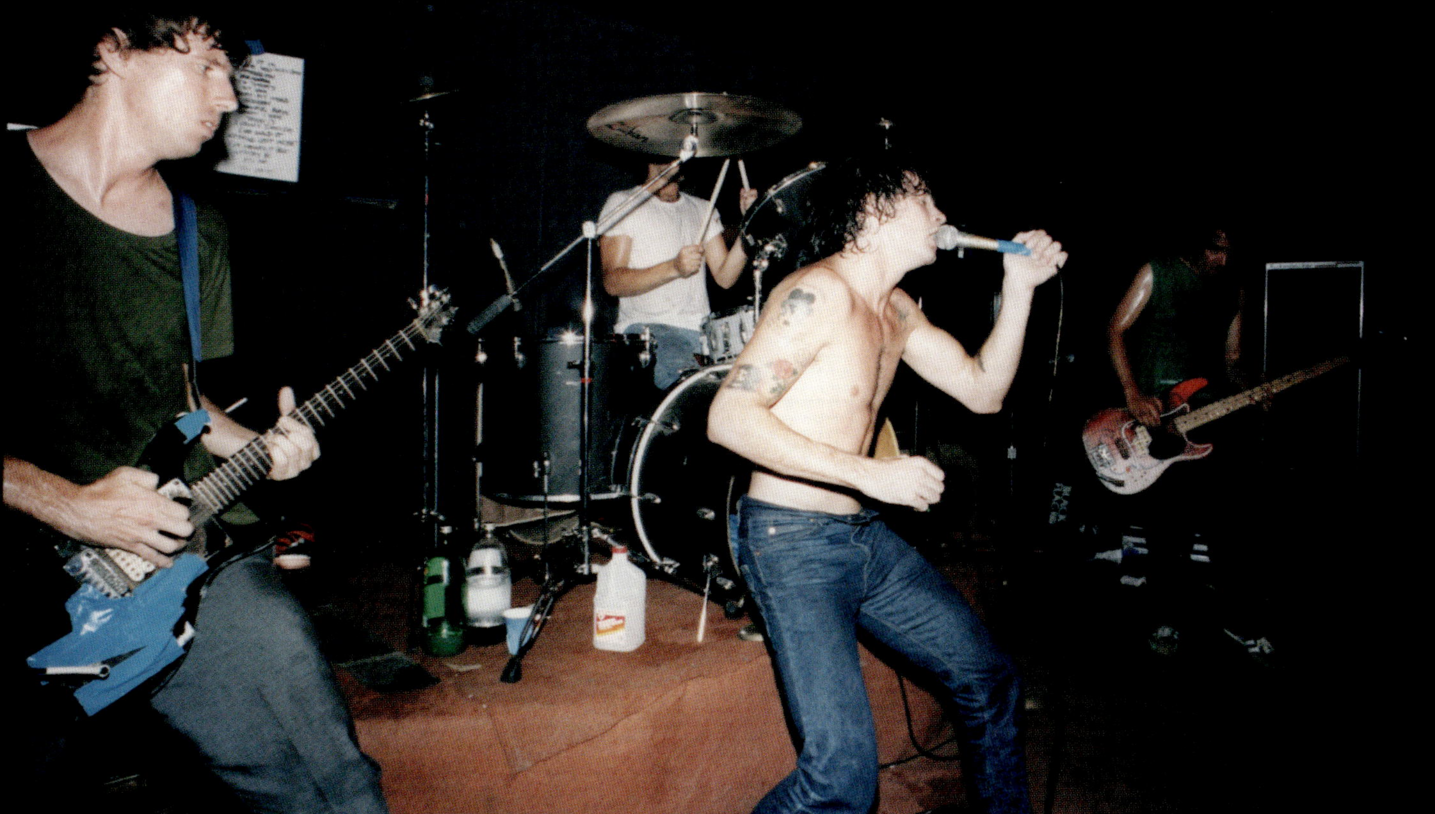

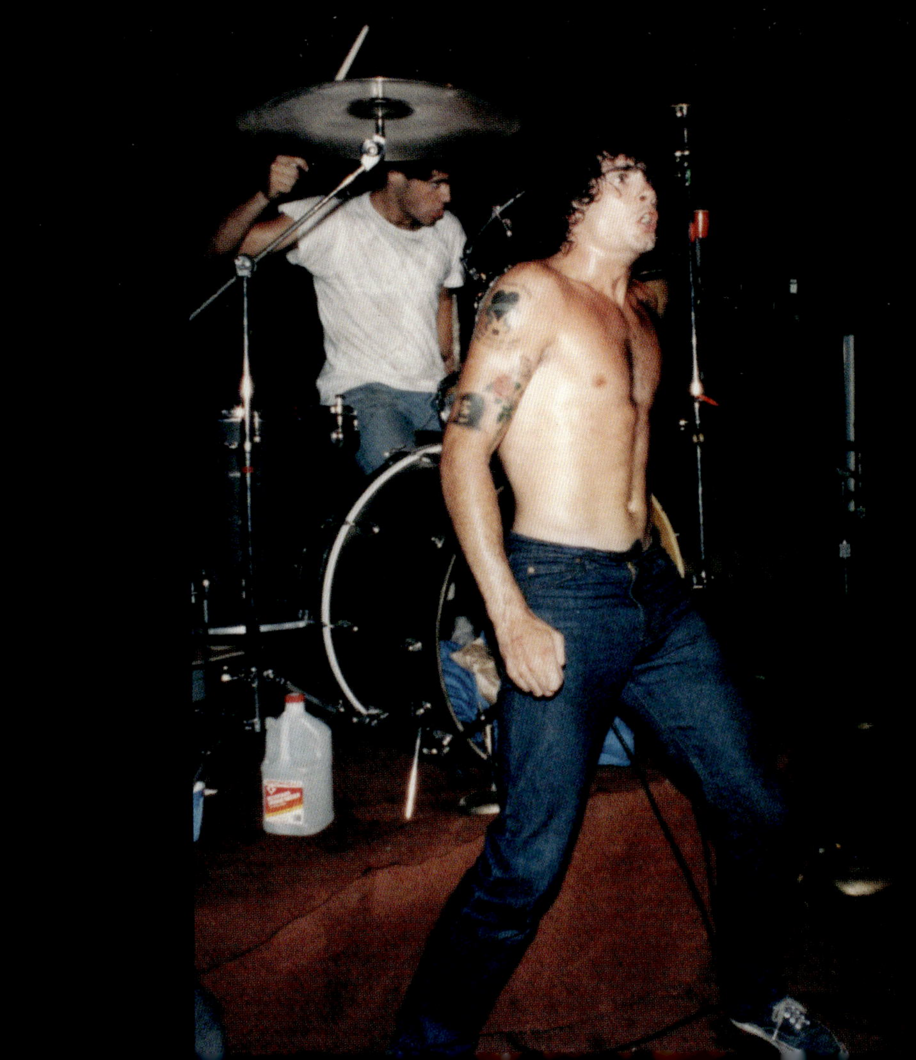
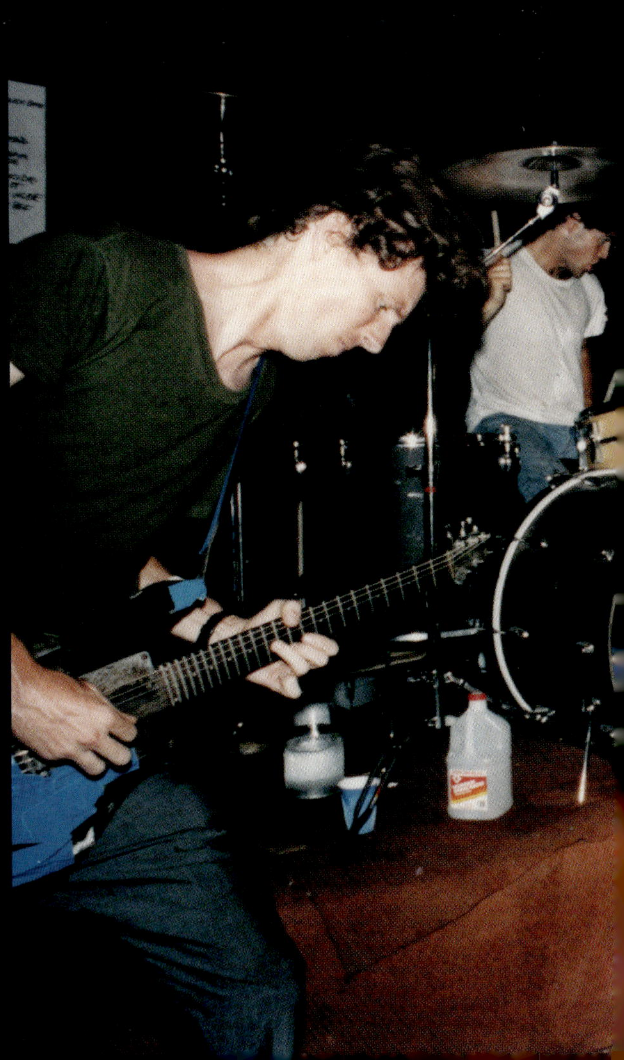

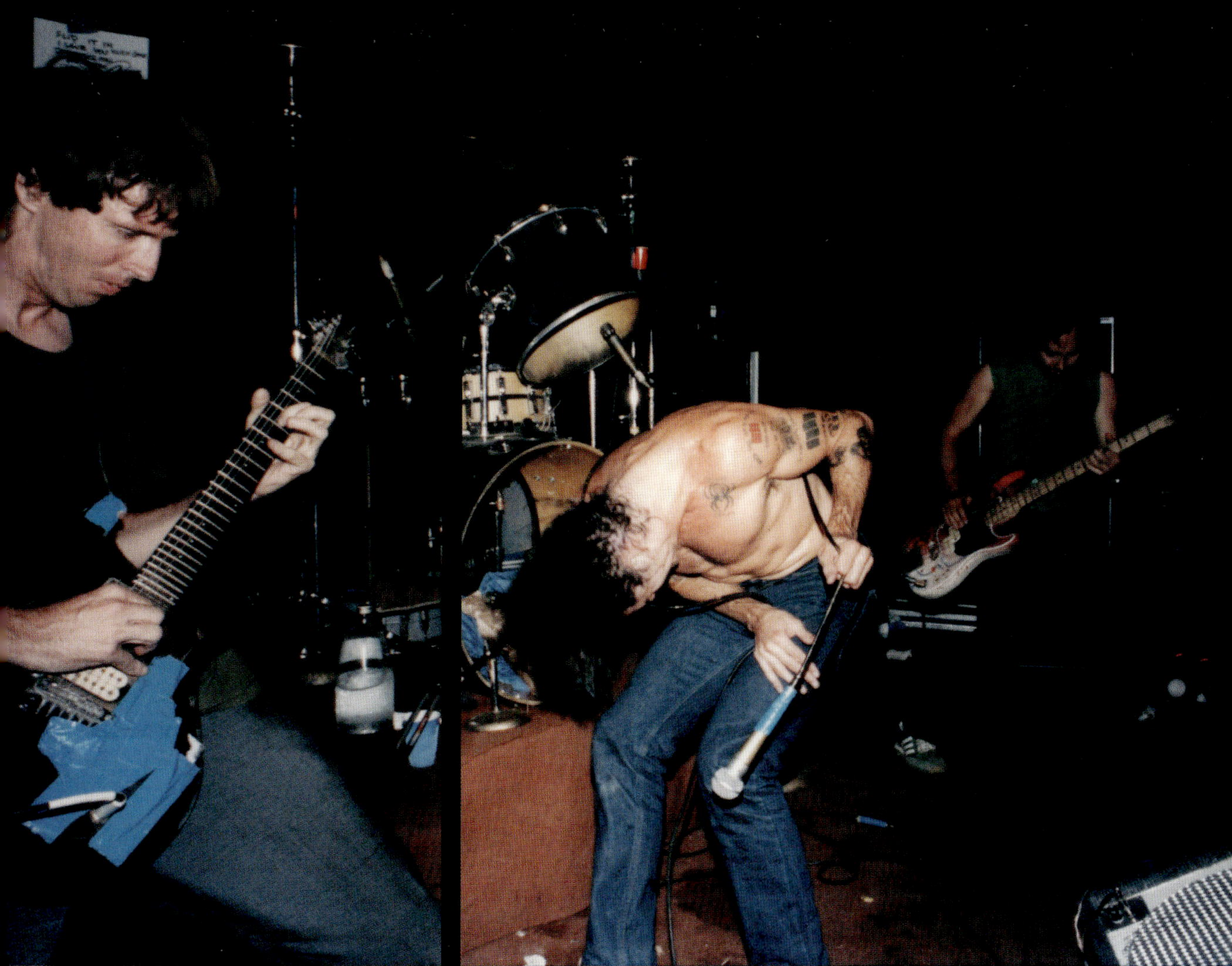

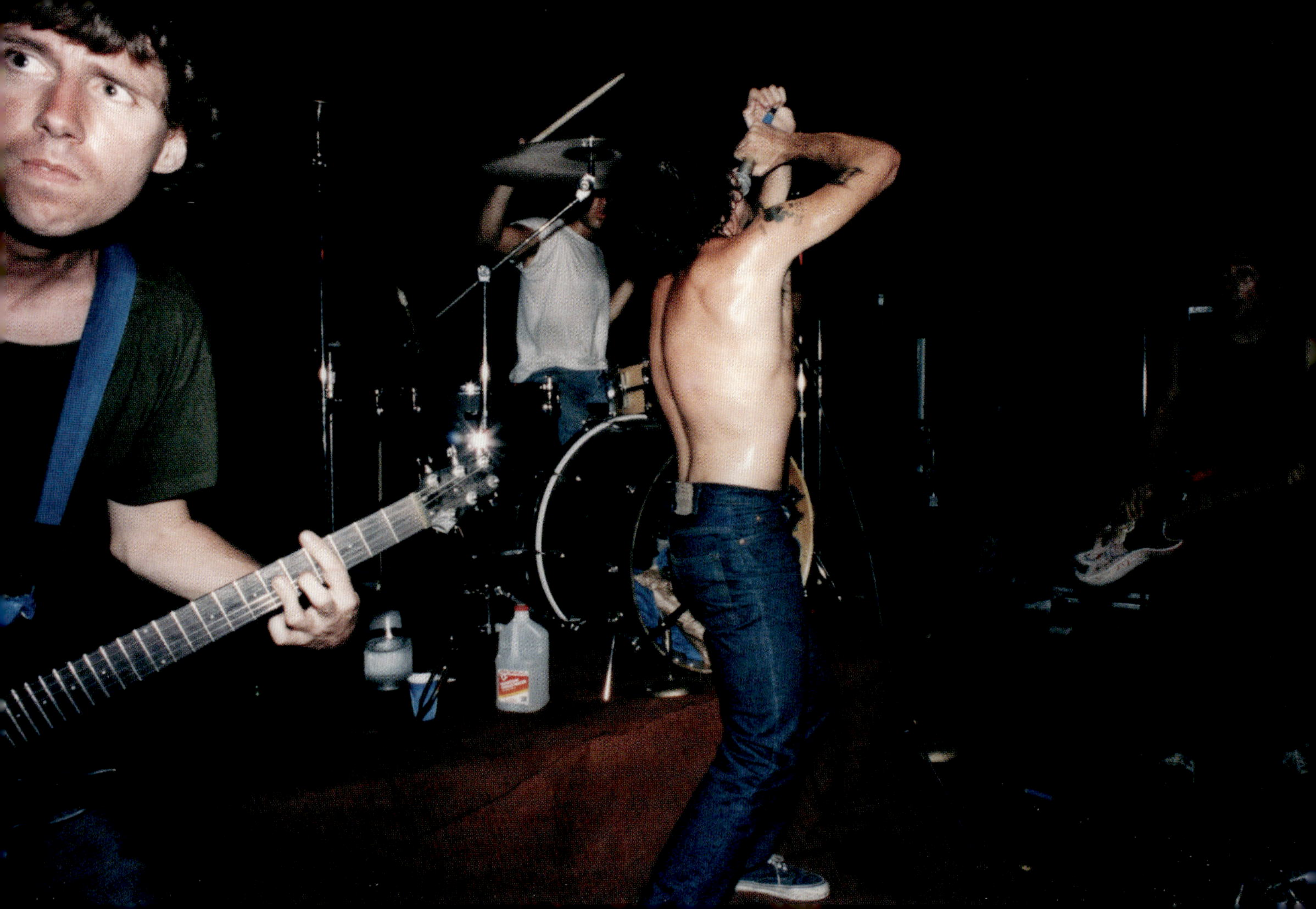

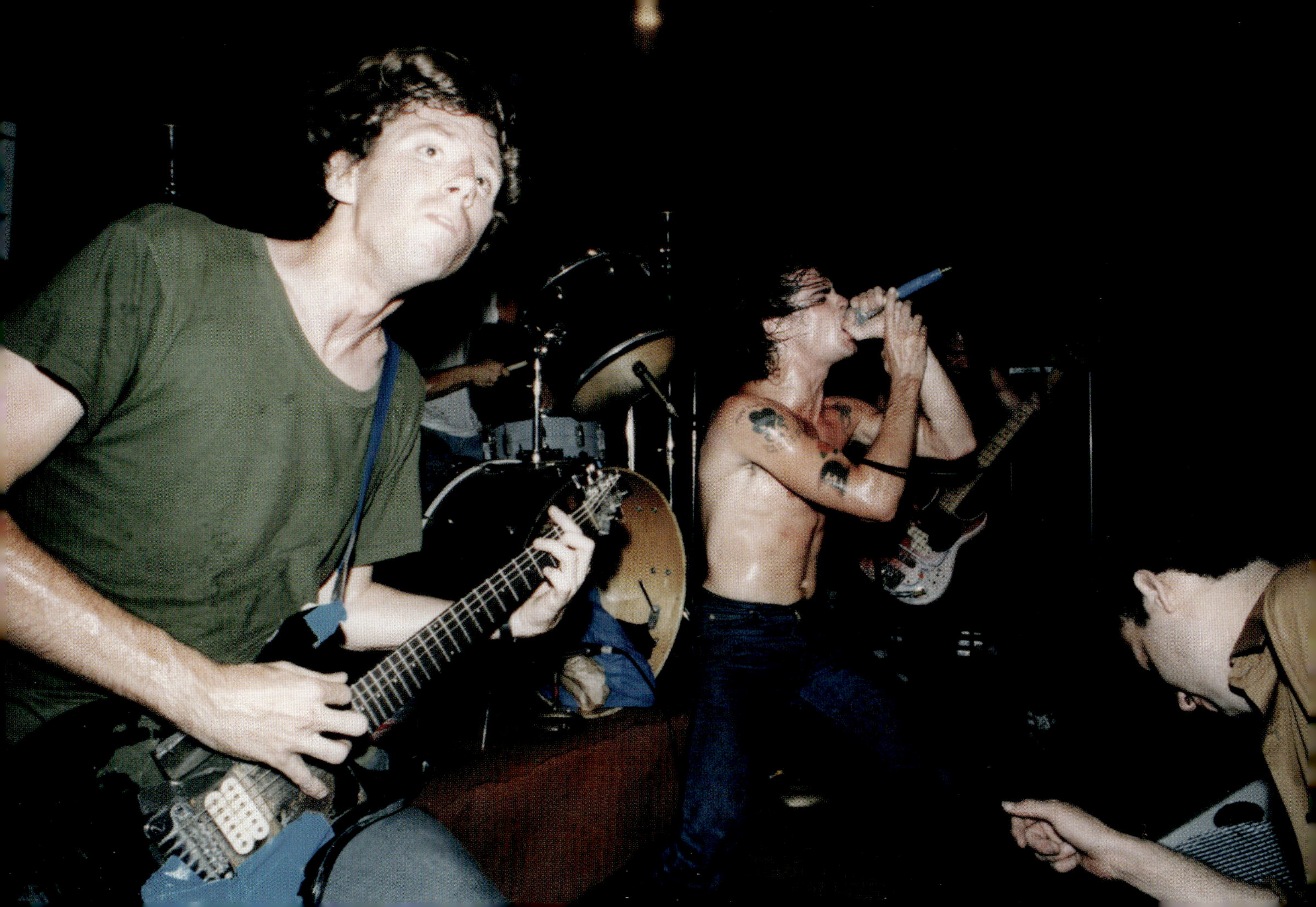

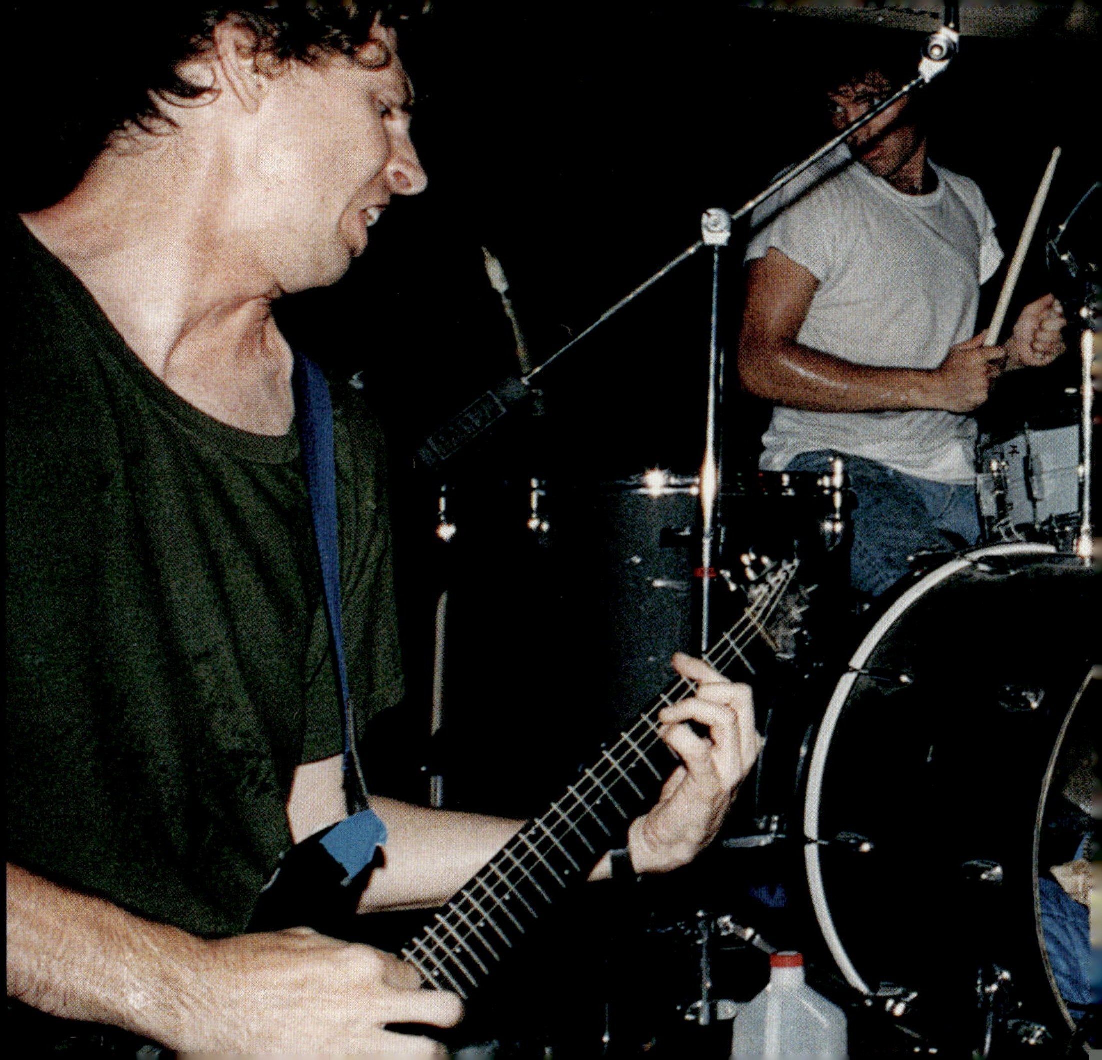

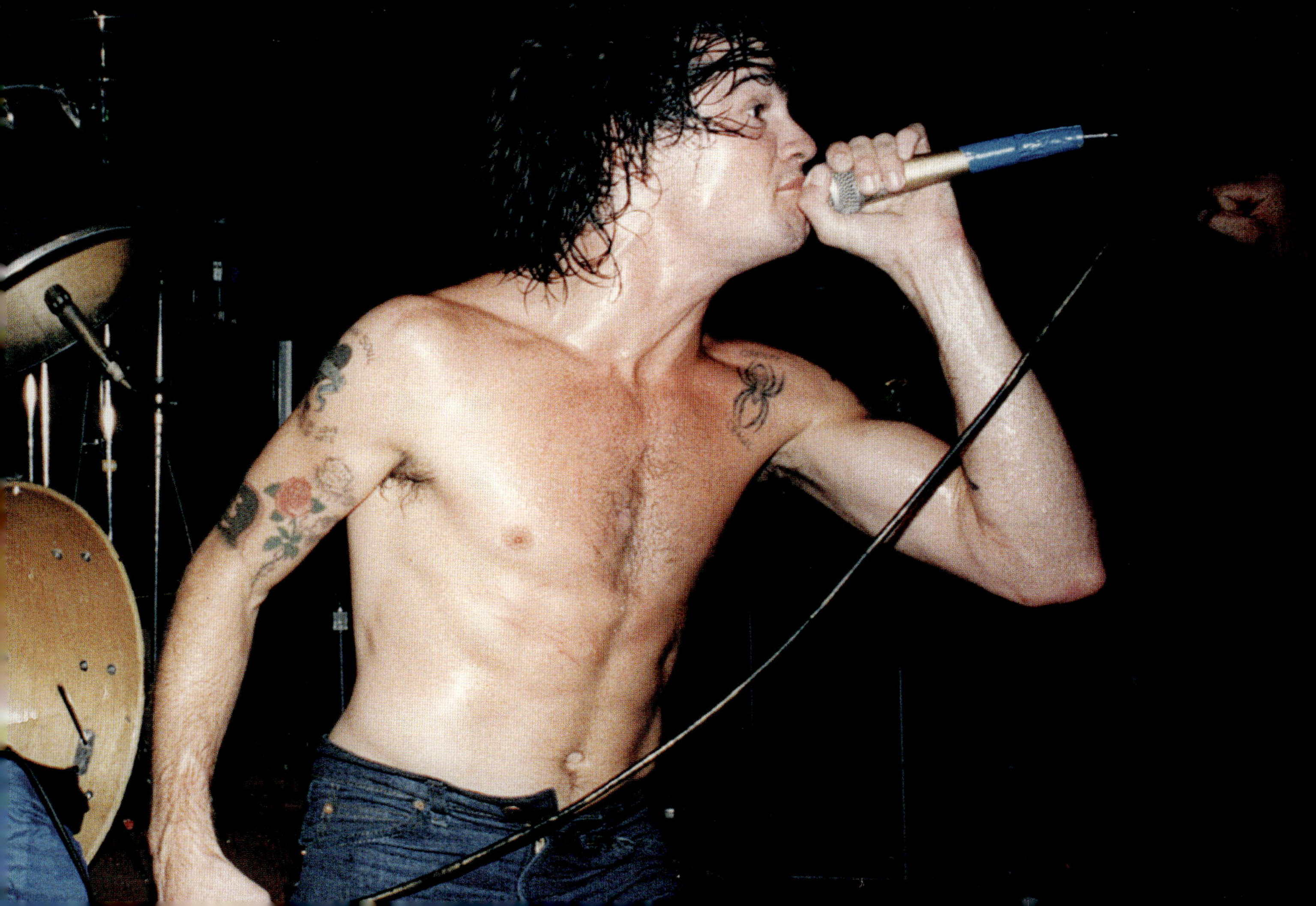

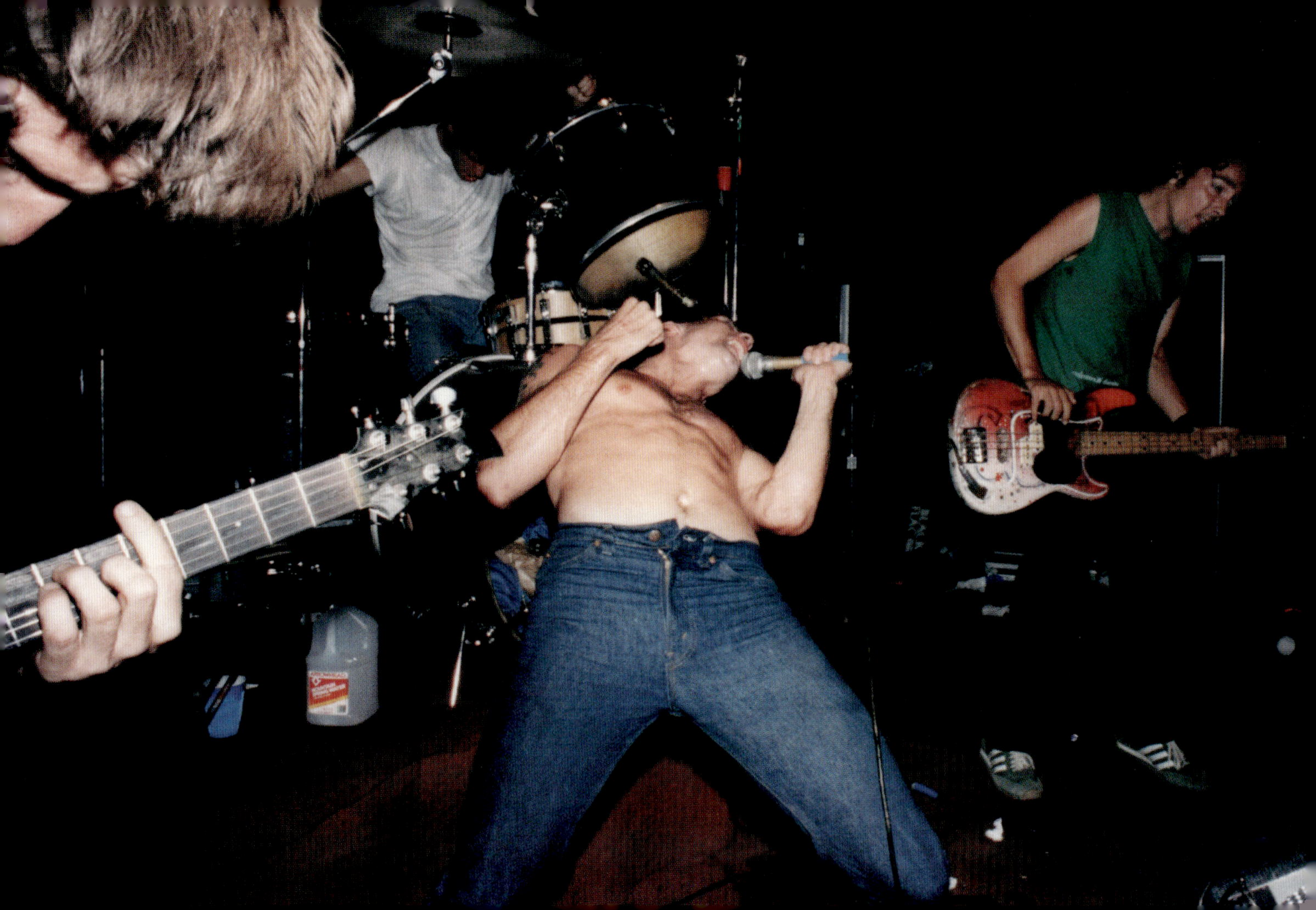

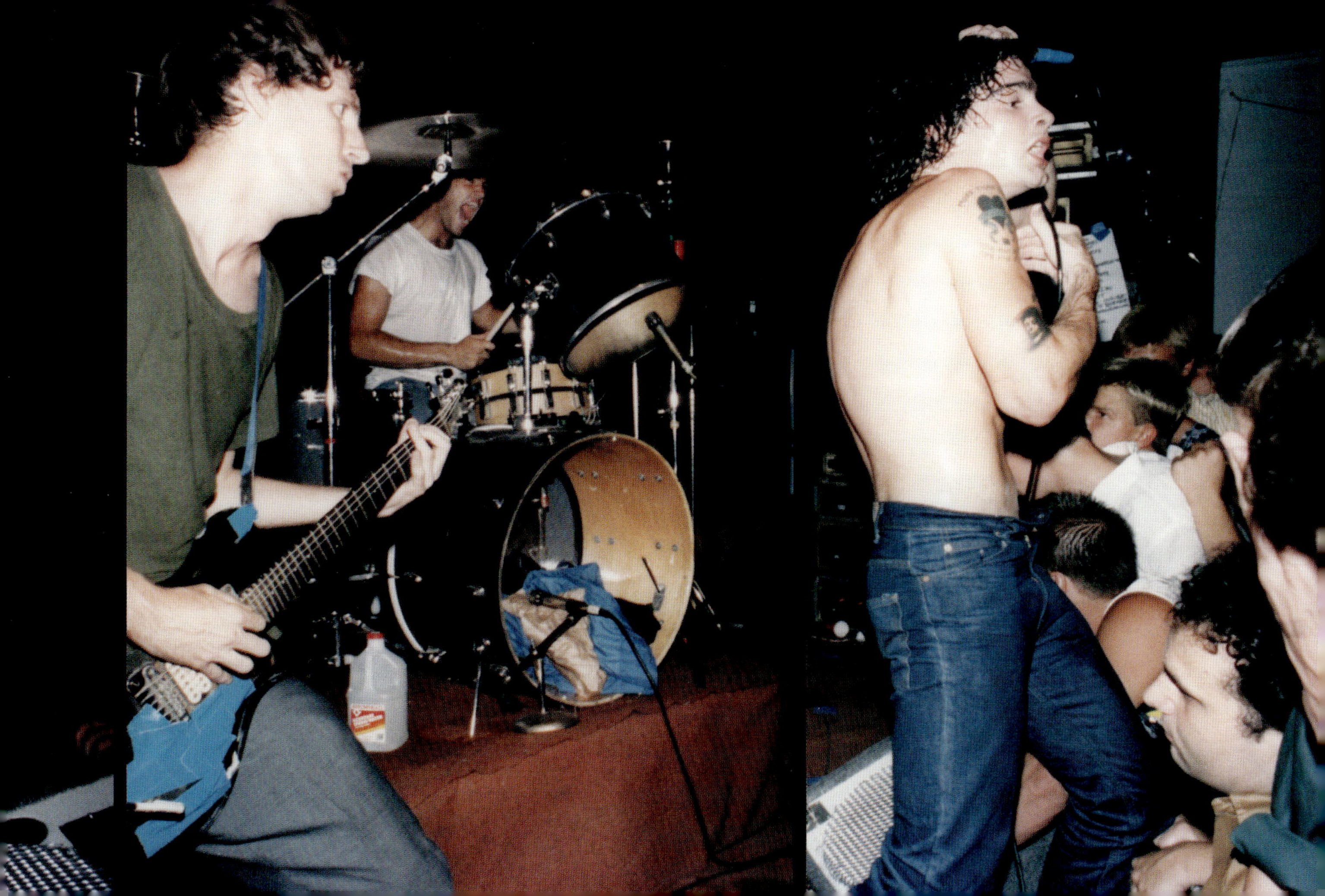

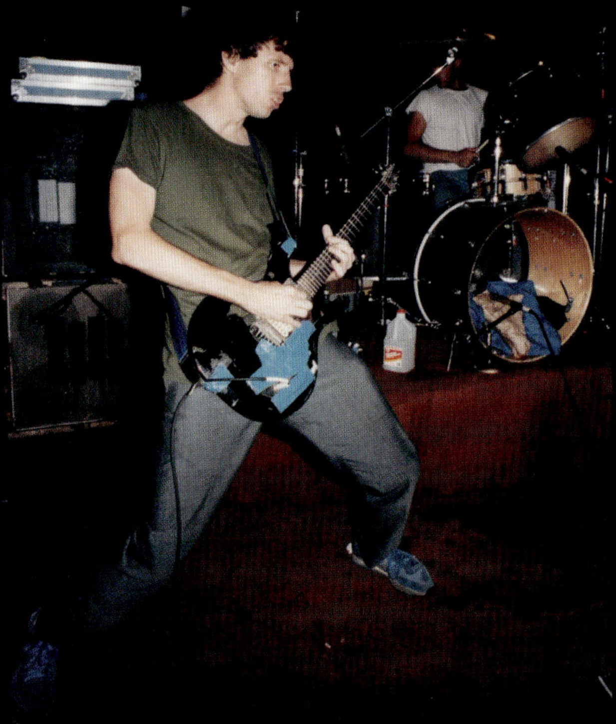

"Something hit the side of my head. All of a sudden I was on the ground trying to get up. The bouncer had hit me in the side of the head when my back was turned. I got to my feet not knowing where I was. He kicked me in the balls and I went down again. I was trying to get up and I saw that he had his knife out and was coming towards me. He was screaming, 'I'll kill you, you fucking punker' I got up and put my hands in front of me. It occurred to me that I was going to get stabbed. His friends tack-wrestled the knife away, just like some movie. The promoter came out of the office and told the guy to leave. The rest of the security guys laughed at me. My face started to swell pretty bad. Hell, that was only the first night. We had to come back and play this fucking dump again the next night."—Henry Rollins, *GET IN THE VAN*

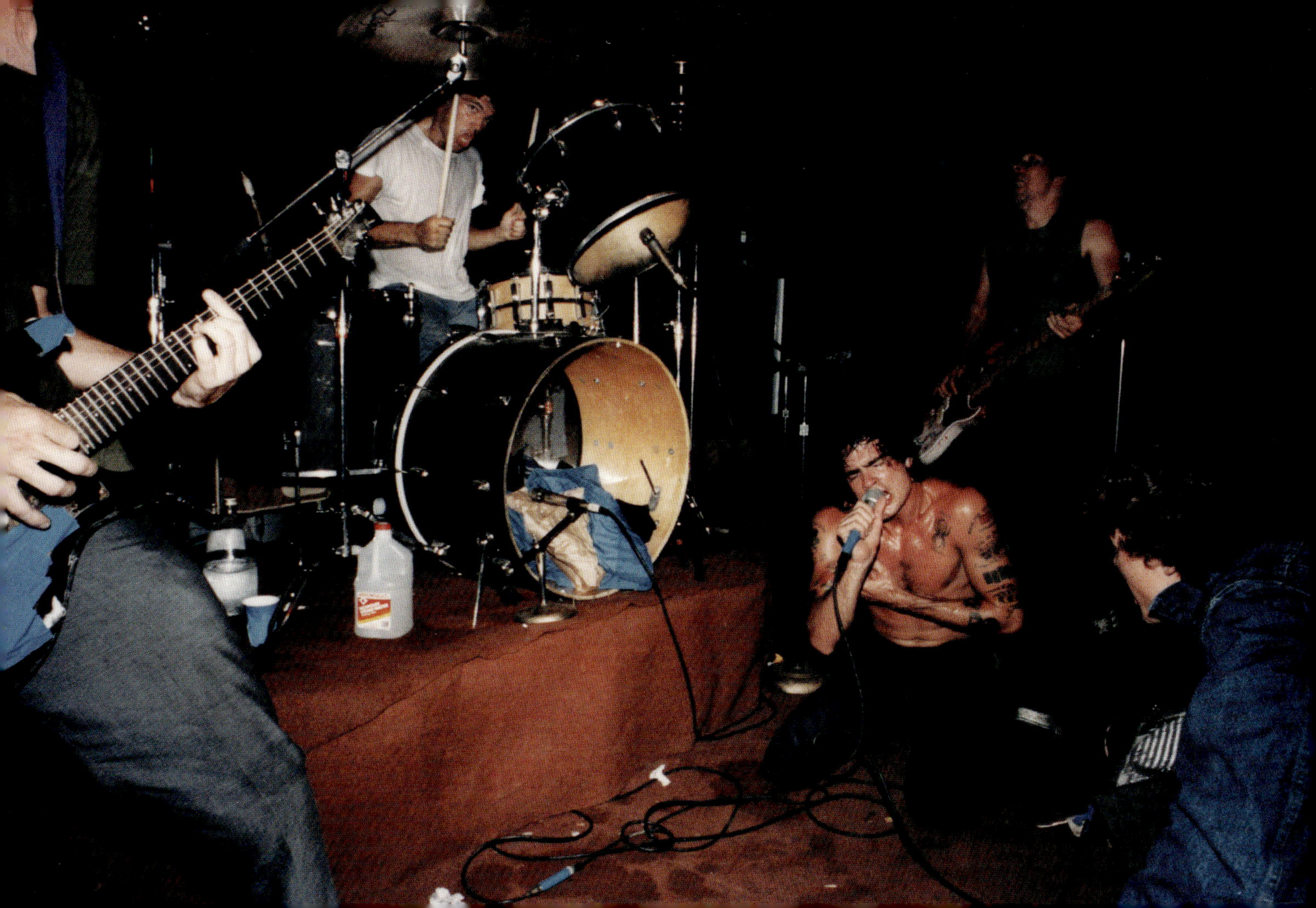

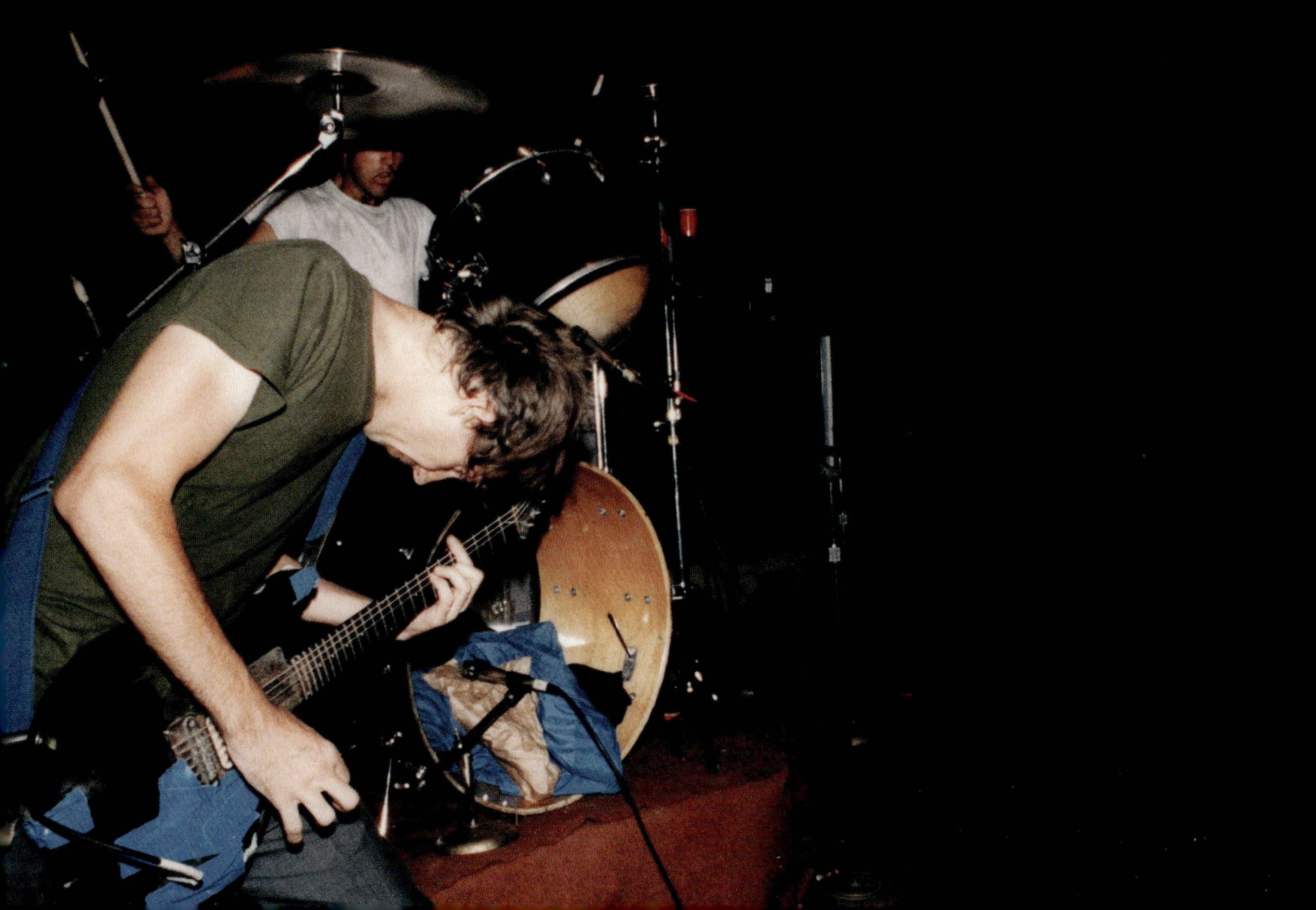

THE VEX : JULY 23, 1983

Slip It In

Black Coffee

I Love You

Depression

TV Party

My War

Beat My Head Against the Wall

Scream

Jealous Again

What I See

Room 13

I Can't Decide

I've Had It

Nothing Left Inside

I've Heard It Before

Nervous Breakdown

Fix Me

Six Pack

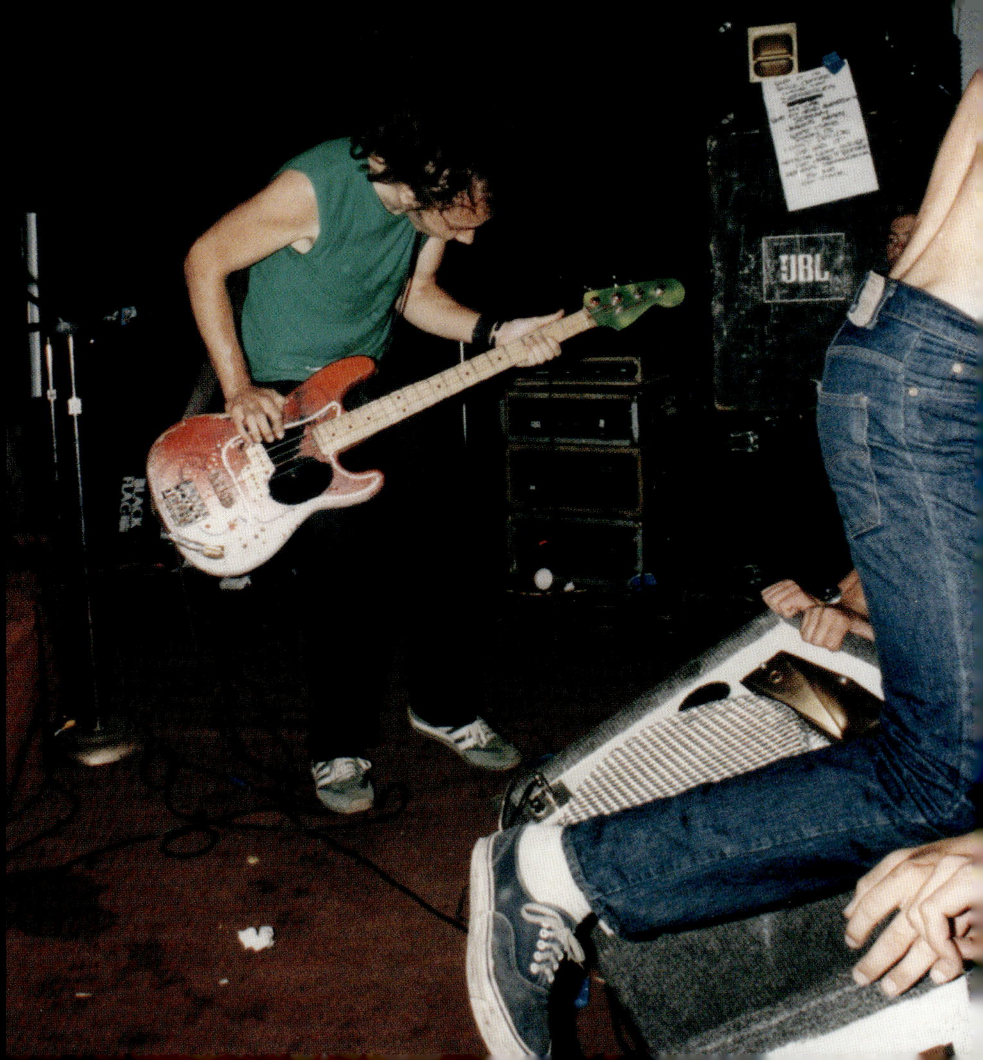

GIMME GIMME GIMME BAZILLION POINTS

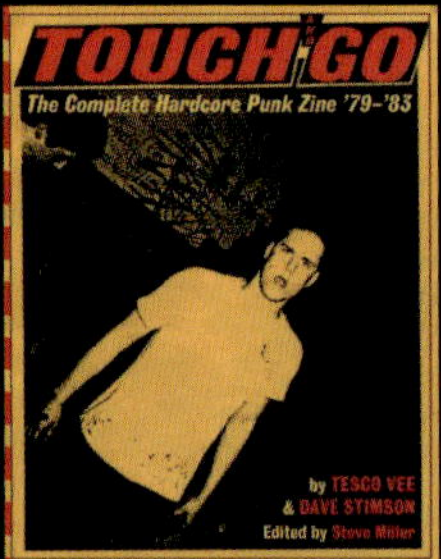

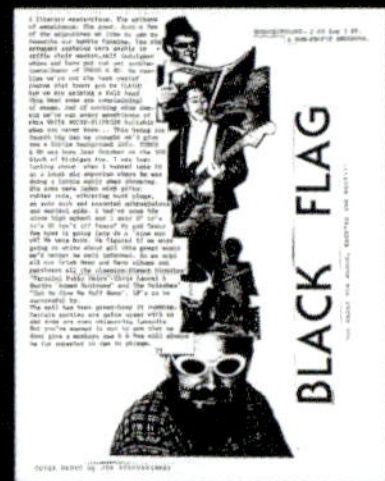

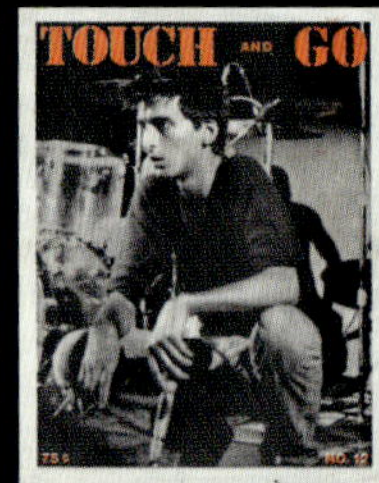

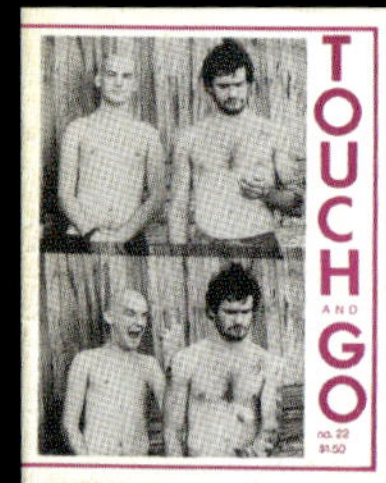

TOUCH AND GO: The Complete Hardcore Punk Zine '79-'83, by Tesco Vee & DS
576pp flexbound | Blow-by-blow hardcore punk as it happened; the complete legendary U.S. zine reprint with new writing by Henry Rollins, Keith Morris, John Brannon, Ian MacKaye, and others.

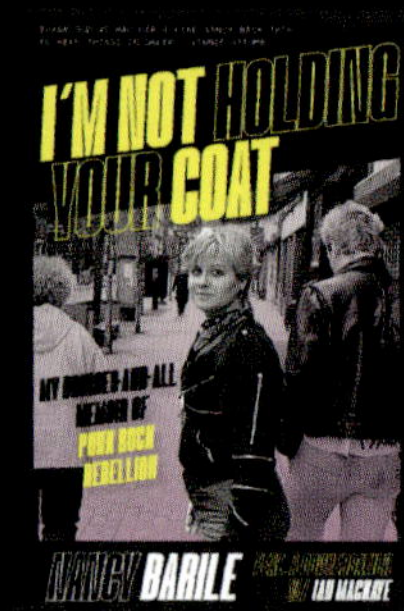

I'M NOT HOLDING YOUR COAT: My Bruises-and-All Memoir of Punk Rock Rebellion, by Nancy Barile
192pp softcover | Crucial front-row view of women in early hardcore punk with Ian MacKaye preface

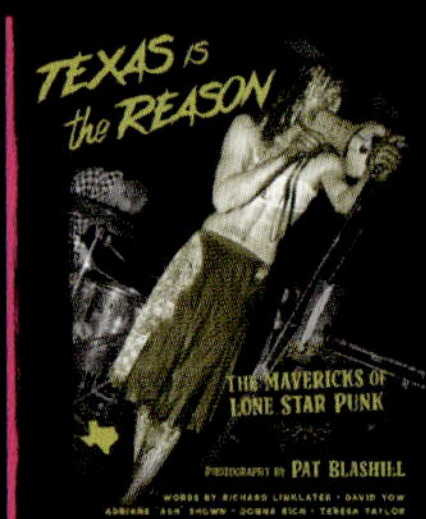

TEXAS IS THE REASON: The Mavericks of Lone Star Punk, by Pat Blashill
240pp hardcover
Photos of the 1980s Austin/San Antonio stampede, w/ Richard Linklater, Teresa Nervosa, David Yow, the Dicks, Big Boys, Butthole Surfers, the Offenders

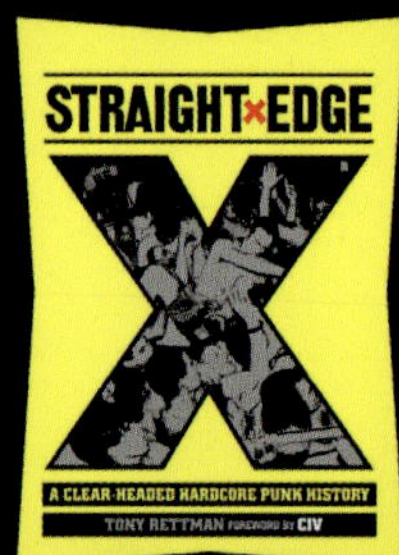

STRAIGHT EDGE: A Clear-Headed Hardcore Punk History, by Tony Rettman, foreword by CIV
400pp softcover | Straight-edge oral history as told by members of Minor Threat, Uniform Choice, SSD, Youth of Today,

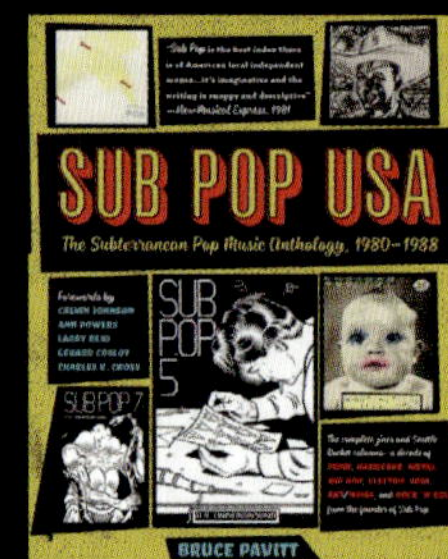

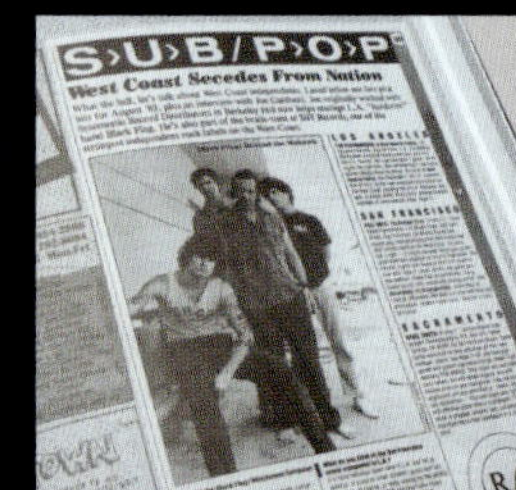

SUB POP USA: The Sub Pop Music Anthology 1980-1988, by Bruce Pavitt | 576pp flexbound | A decade of DIY writing on 1,000 independent bands from the cofounder of Sub Pop Records

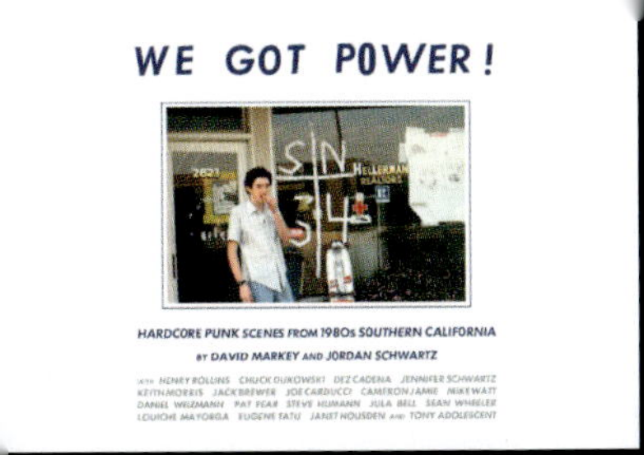

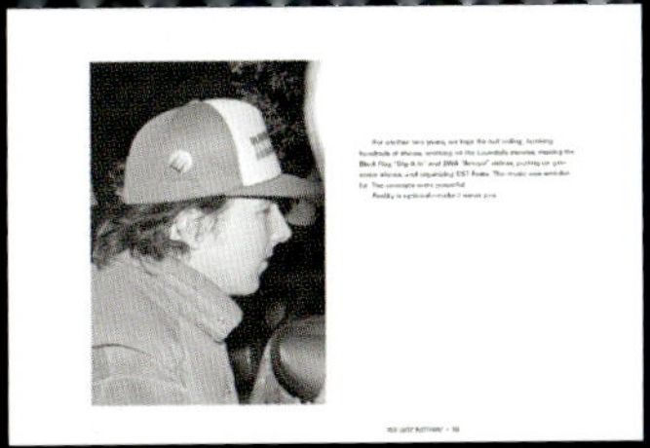

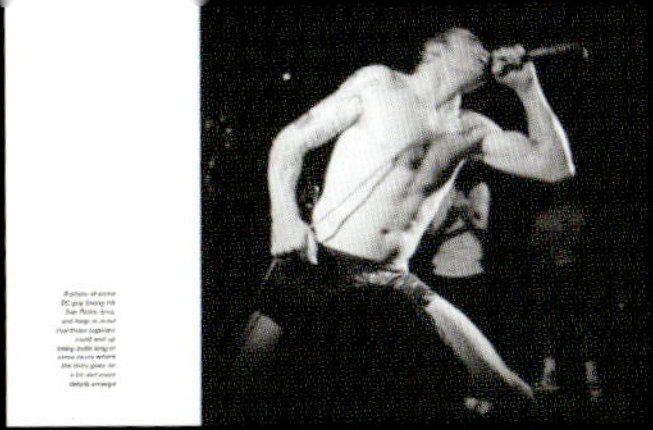

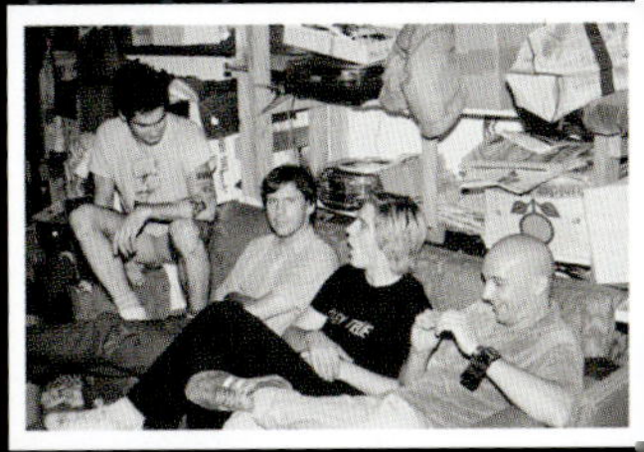

WE GOT POWER!: Hardcore Punk Scenes from 1980s Southern California by David Markey & Jordan Schwartz
288pp hardcover | 400 photos | Massive essays by four Black Flag members, plus players from Suicidal Tendencies, Circle Jerks, Saccharine Trust, Mike Watt, Redd Kross, the Vandals, and color zine reprints. *Party with us, punker!*

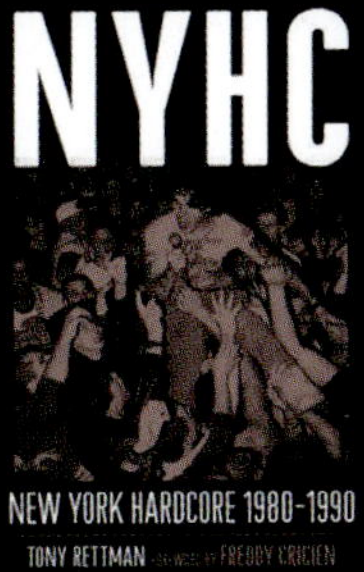

NYHC: New York Hardcore, 1980–1990, by Tony Rettman, foreword by Freddy Cricien | 384pp softcover CBGB matinee mania w/Agnostic Front, Cro-Mags, Gorilla Biscuits, Warzone, Bad Brains, Murphy's Law, Stimulators, Sick of It All

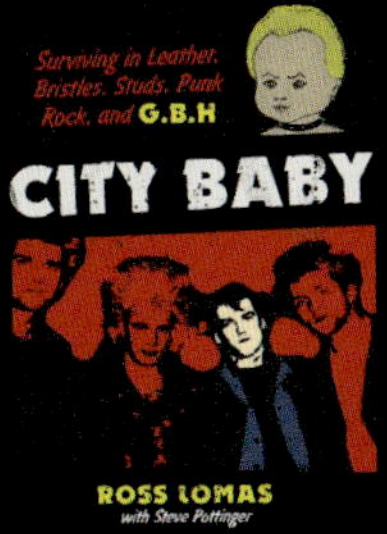

CITY BABY: Surviving in Leather, Bristles, Studs, Punk Rock, and G.B.H., by Ross Lomas
204pp softcover | Decades of hilarious punk mayhem lived by G.B.H.'s indestructible bassist

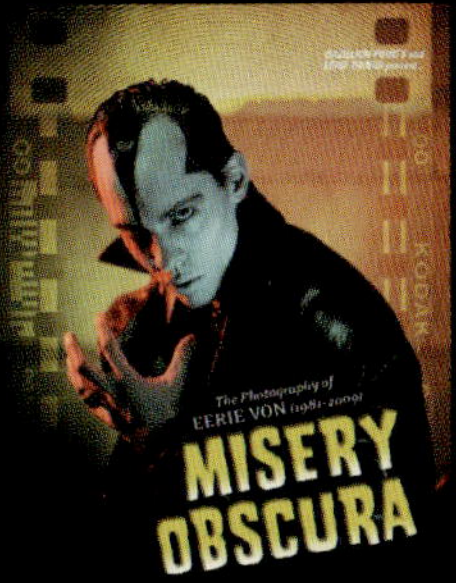

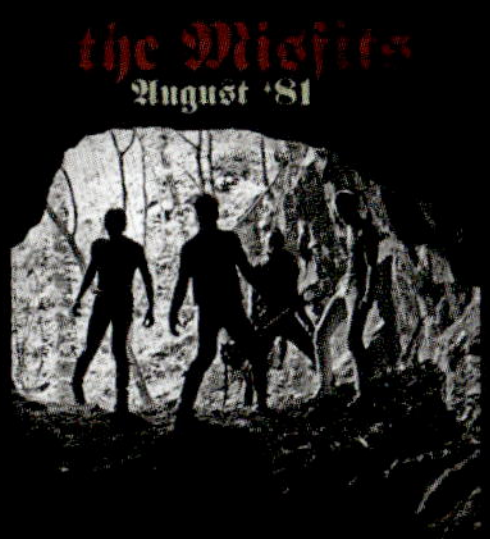

MISERY OBSCURA: The Photography of Eerie Von, by Eerie Von, foreword by Lyle Preslar | 160pp hardcover
Fiendish photos by Misfits/Samhain/Danzig mainstay

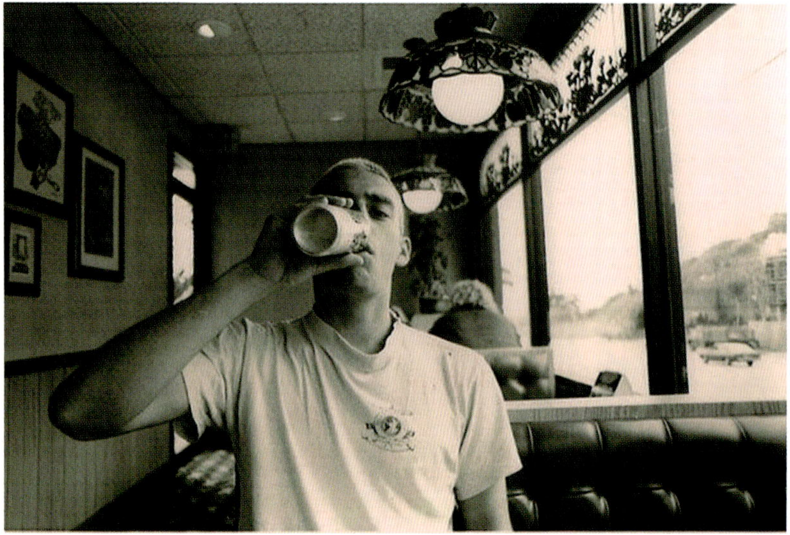

MICHAEL PEARSON

The author pounding a Schlitz Bull Tall at Jack in the Box on Sunset Blvd. near Pacific Coast Highway, 1983

ACKNOWLEDGMENTS

Thank you to my mom and dad, Ben and Jean, who let me go to punk shows from an early age, and permitted me to play punk music in the garage, driving them and the neighbors crazy. Thanks to my wife Bita, and my kids Benjamin and Daniel. And thanks to the aging—and deceased—punkers whose love of this unique music carries on and is reflected in every young new face in the crowd.

Many thanks to Ian Christe for seeing how this could become a cool book and a lasting document of a special moment in punk rock: Black Flag in 1983 at these two great shows. His vision, thoughtfulness, and hard work made this happen. I'm also grateful to Black Flag for putting every ounce of their energy into their music and performances; you can see their unbelievable intensity in the photos. Much appreciation to David Jones for helping me to describe in words this phase of Black Flag, the *My War* era. And thanks to myself for not losing or wrecking these photos over the last forty years !!!

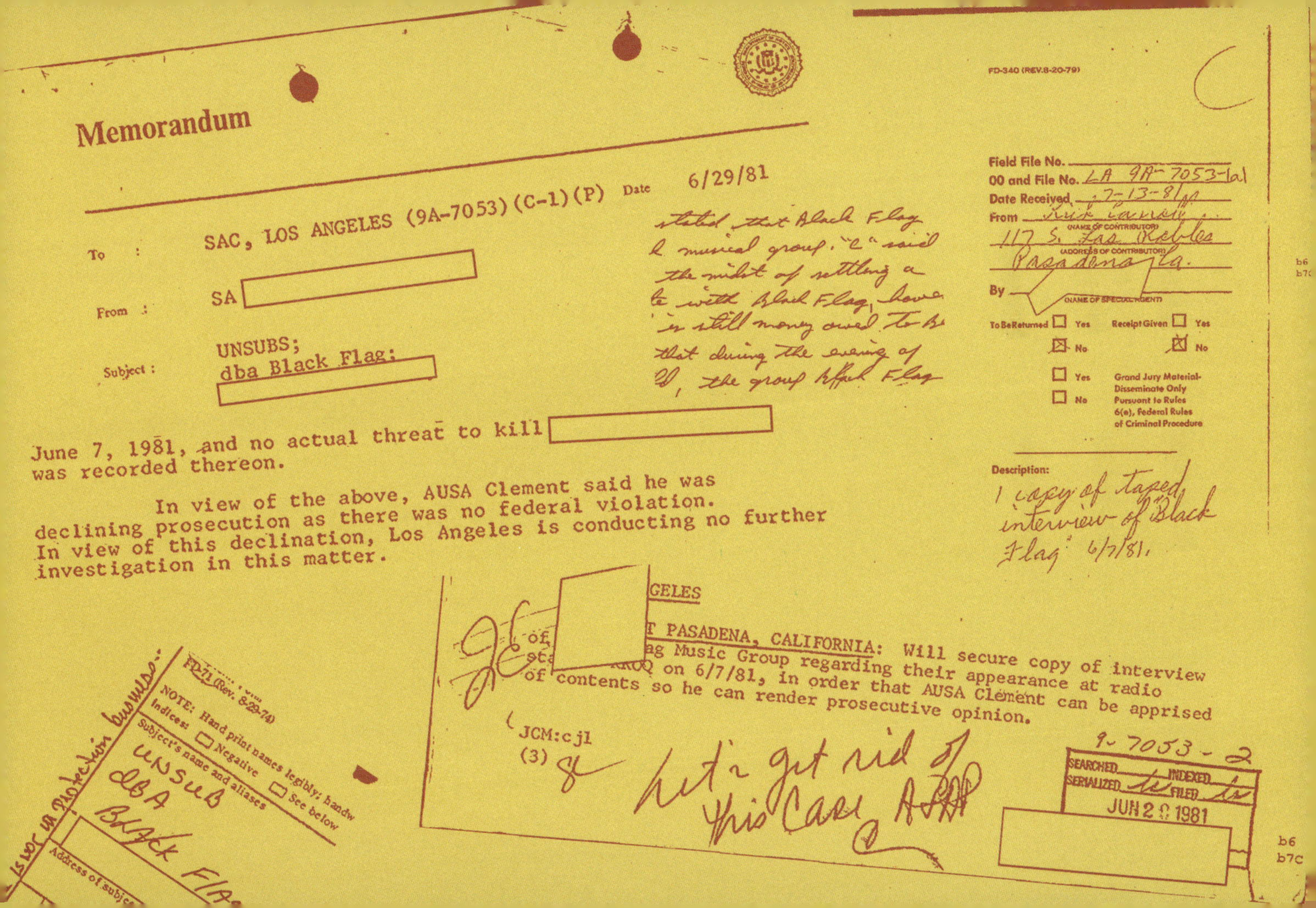

FD-340 (REV.8-20-79)

Memorandum

To : SAC, LOS ANGELES (9A-7053)(C-1)(P) Date 6/29/81

From : SA [redacted]

Subject : UNSUBS;
dba Black Flag;

stated that Black Flag
a musical group. "C" said
the midst of settling a
with Black Flag, however
is still money owed to Bl
that during the evening of
the group Black Flag

June 7, 1981, and no actual threat to kill [redacted]
was recorded thereon.

In view of the above, AUSA Clement said he was declining prosecution as there was no federal violation. In view of this declination, Los Angeles is conducting no further investigation in this matter.

Field File No.
00 and File No. LA 9A-7053-1a1
Date Received 7-13-81
From [redacted] (NAME OF CONTRIBUTOR)
117 S. Las Robles (ADDRESS OF CONTRIBUTOR)
Pasadena Ca.
By [redacted] (NAME OF SPECIAL AGENT)

To Be Returned ☐ Yes ☒ No
Receipt Given ☐ Yes ☒ No
☐ Yes ☐ No Grand Jury Material-Disseminate Only Pursuant to Rules 6(e), Federal Rules of Criminal Procedure

Description:
1 copy of taped interview of "Black Flag" 6/7/81.

b6
b7C

[redacted] GELES

[redacted] T PASADENA, CALIFORNIA: Will secure copy of interview of [redacted] ag Music Group regarding their appearance at radio sta[redacted] KROQ on 6/7/81, in order that AUSA Clement can be apprised of contents so he can render prosecutive opinion.

JCM:cjl
(3)

Let's get rid of this case ASAP

9-7053-2
SEARCHED INDEXED
SERIALIZED FILED
JUN 2 ? 1981

b6
b7C

FD-71 (Rev. 8-29-74)
NOTE: Hand print names legibly; handw
Indices: ☐ Negative ☐ See below
Subject's name and aliases
UNSUB
dBA
Black Flag
Address of subject

Is not in Protection business.

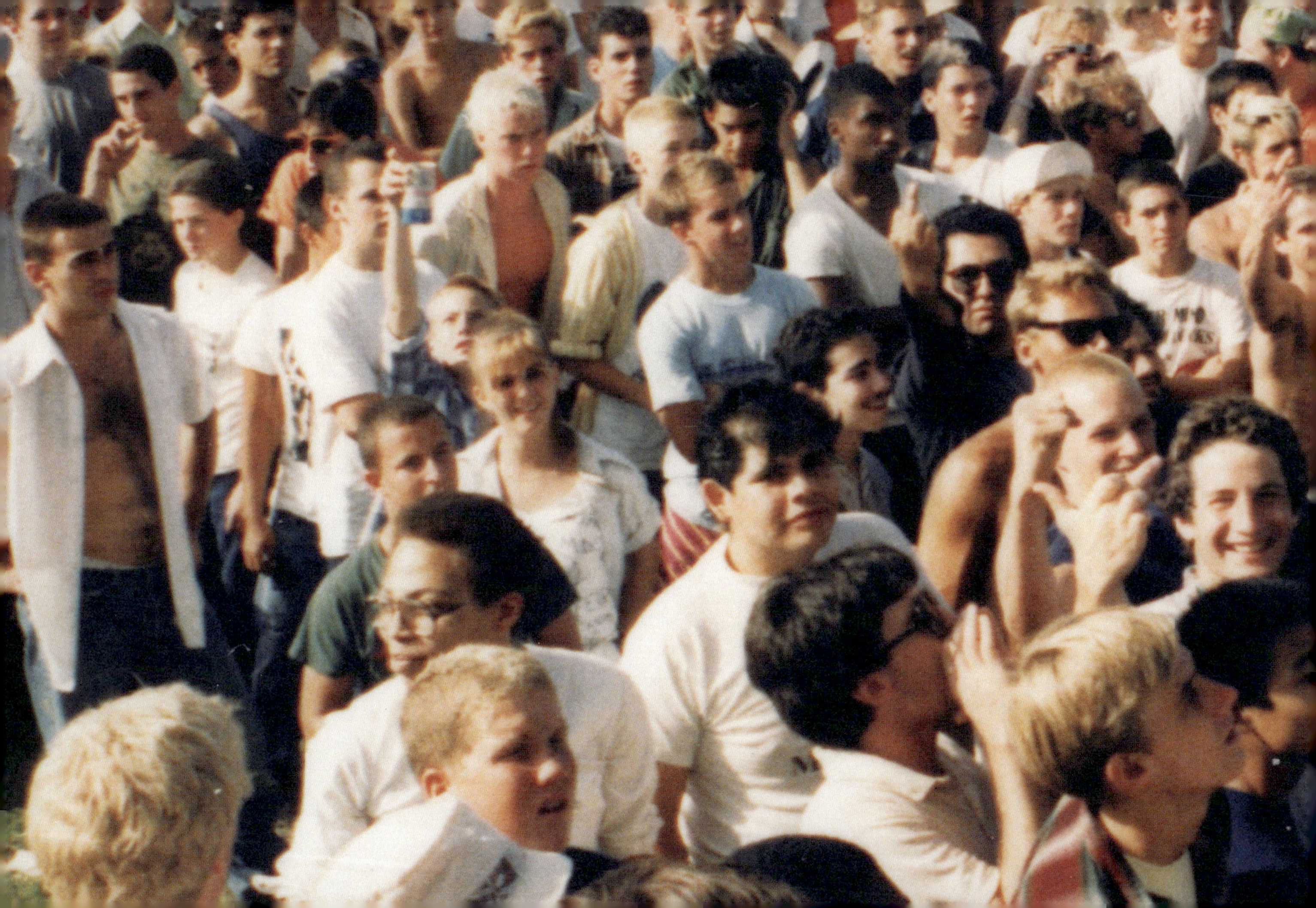